CREOSOTE RAIN

A carnival kid's quest for home, family, and belonging.

By Joe Makston

Joe Makston

Independent Publisher
Phoenix Arizona

Cover design: Viktorjia Celikovic
Editor: Susanne Schotanus from Passionate Writer Coaching
Copyeditor: Celina Rhodes
Book Formatting: Manuel Quintana

ISBN: 979-8-218-24458-3
eISBN:978-1-0882-1782-5

For Joey, my younger self. Your voice matters. I see you. I love you. Thank you for taking care of me for so many years.

Table of Contents

Preface

Thank you for picking up this book. It contains a roller coaster ride of ups and downs as I try to find a sense of belonging in the world. I hope you'll laugh at the lighter moments and at least understand, maybe even relate to, why life has been so complicated for me.

When I first started thinking about writing this book, I really wanted to understand the reason behind it. Why would anyone want to read this particular story? There are plenty out there, what's so special about mine that could motivate one to read my experiences? Then, I realized we all have something to share with the world. My story, like so many, starts with a traumatic childhood that I spent the next decades coming to terms with. This story gives a voice to the inner chatter of young Joey, sharing the experience of a lonely boy, growing up in a carnival, having a divorced family in the 80's, being different from the other boys, finding a community – and the effects of all of this. This book may resonate differently with one person than another, but that's the beauty of life; it's not one size fits all. We hear things differently, and we experience life in a variety of ways. Then, as the sun sets on the days, years, and decades of life, we can have a moment to reflect on the legacy we left. My hope is that Joey's voice is heard and comforting to your younger self.

As I've reflected on these stories, I found moments of shame, judgment, and unkindness. It took years of therapy and choosing to think differently before I realized who I was and did the work to become who I am today. I'm certainly a work in progress just ask my kids! haha. But I'm healthier for having done the work, and for continuing to do it day in and day out. There are also things I'm thankful to celebrate, like being a good dad, a reliable friend, a storyteller, a mentor, and a damn good-looking guy. (Okay, that last one is wishful thinking.) At the end of the day, I want Joey to be proud of who he was and who he is now. There's no need to hide any part of who he is at his core; he can love deeply and receive the same love in return.

I've spent most of my life showing people that someone cares about them. I couldn't put words to it early on, but now when people ask "who is Joe Makston?" I can honestly say that I want people to know it through my words and actions. It's funny how this is innately part of who I am, as I often felt like the odd man out in family, friends, and even church. I was constantly anxious about it and tried very hard to be the kind of person people would be willing to accept. My intention was and always has been to connect people to a community where they have a sense of belonging and can be their whole selves. But I didn't really feel like I belonged, despite my best efforts. This book is the result of trying, failing, then trying again, in the hopes that I can give you the sense of acceptance and wholeness that you might also long for.

As you read *Creosote Rain*, I encourage you to consider your own history of resilience, failure, and hopefully, healing. These are difficult stories to write and maybe equally difficult for you to read. If you've experienced domestic violence, any form of abuse, abandonment, or neglect, please be aware some stories could be triggering. Make sure you have a support system or talk with a licensed therapist to help you heal from that trauma.

Thank you for going on this journey of moving out of a desolate place, through the storms, to be refreshed by the fragrance of *Creosote Rain*. Okay, let's get the shit show started. Hold on and keep your hands and feet inside the car while the ride is moving. See you on the other side.

Without further ado, here is *Creosote Rain*.

Introduction

The desert of Tucson, Arizona, was a barren land, thirsty for water to nourish the roots of cacti and desert scrub. Summers held back life with clenched hands. Dust devils twirled through the air like a spinning ice skater, scooping up the slightly sifted layers of dust, crafting brown funnels that danced across the open landscape. Then the billowing cloud would fall as the funnel broke, until the sky would seem to inhale all the wind again, leaving a stale, motionless field caked in its own brown soot.

Before the sun got too high, early mornings would give way to the wildlife greeting each other as they searched for food. Roadrunners, lizards, field mice, and horned toads scurried through their well-worn trailways before the sun began beating. It was a sun-scorched scene of withering plants and small puffs of dust clouds with every step we took running, playing cops and robbers, shooting BB guns, chasing rabbits, or trying to find a hiding spot behind a scraggly bush.

My brother, Pat, and I got used to seeing the parched land as we headed out to play during long summer days. We'd pack a bologna sandwich, so we could explore as far as we wanted. Desert fields connected one neighborhood to another, allowing us to move through the city without even going on a street. As the sun would get high in the day, we'd find shelter in a fast-food joint to ask for cups of water and then head back to continue exploring. Our sunburns were badges of honor that reflected our adventures through riverbeds and fields from the previous day.

Midway through summer, the weather would begin to change, bringing on the monsoon season. Thunderhead clouds would begin to form just over the mountains, folding in on themselves, doubling in size in minutes, thrusting another cloud full of rain into existence. Thunder was our queue to get out of the riverbeds because water was coming soon, even if it wasn't raining where we were. The air that had been stagnant for days began to move, bringing the scent of creosote into my nostrils. Creosote is a desert bush that releases a fragrant woodsy scent into the air when it gets wet. When I was a kid, people would say "smells like rain." That is actually the smell of wet creosote. The scent cued to us, the wildlife and desert that a nourishing rain was coming.

When the first drops started to fall, we would brace for the short downpour from the thunderous and lightning-filled clouds that hugged Mt. Lemmon. The showers quickly grew from little droplets to a water hose on full blast, dousing our skin with cool strokes of water. As the rain subsided, streets overflowed with the residue of dirty water which raced down each side, making its way to the brimming storm drains. The scent of freshly poured rain would again permeate my nostrils with the fragrance of creosote bushes. The once barren, thirsty desert slowly transformed into a refreshed landscape of plants heavy with raindrops being routed to their emaciated roots. The desert would seem to stand more upright, breathing a refreshing sigh as it was strengthened by the rainfall and nitrogen deposited by the lightning storm. The wildlife emerged from their resting places and surveyed pools of water to lap up a drink.

The desert is reminiscent of my childhood; dry, desolate, and longing to be nurtured. It's also similar in how it adapts to stay alive, using just enough energy to sustain itself, but never thriving. Although there were moments of great joy, accomplishment, and celebration, I lived in a constant state of neglect and trauma imposed by my mom. This is my story of growing up in an emotionally disconnected family, with parents who didn't have the capacity to take care of us, and the people who stepped in to fill those gaps. My siblings and I are grateful to these men and women who said, "Yes, I will come alongside you." These people were the refreshing 'Creosote Rain' that poured their lives into us, giving much-needed nourishment to our roots, giving us confidence, and comforting our parched souls. They gave us the first glimpses of what it would be like to not just live in a desolate place but thrive despite our circumstances. They gave us a sense of acceptance and belonging. They sacrificed emotionally, financially, and sometimes even physically to show love to and take care of someone else's kids, so we wouldn't get lost in the chaos of living on the fringe of society.

Part One

The Carnie Code

Kathy (Mom) was a five-foot Polish descendant born and raised on a farm in Fairbury, IL. Her signature bleached blond beehive hair gave her at least three more inches of height and made her easy to spot anywhere in a crowd. As a self-proclaimed dumpster diver, she was known to strap a mattress and furniture to the top of her car straight off the side of the road. Mom was a hundred percent hustle in how she worked to put food on the table and a roof over our heads, all the while playing an angle to get what she wanted. She spoke her mind and also knew when to temper it. She always demanded her kids obey one rule, "listen and be good." She has a mouth that can whip you like a cat of nine tails, and her favorite nickname for people is "son of a bitch."

When Mom was sixteen years old, she got pregnant. Since it all happened in a small farm community, the family would have to bear the shame for decades. As a result, Mom was shipped off to Bloomington IL, to have the baby and give it up for adoption. When she returned home, she was told she couldn't live there any longer and was disowned by her mother. She struggled through finishing high school, then started a certified nursing assistant program at the local college. This would ultimately become Mom's career. It was a labor-intensive job, as she would administer meds, move patients around in the bed, help them go to the bathroom, and clean them up.

By the time Mom was twenty-four, she was already in her second marriage. After leaving her son with his dad and collecting her two daughters, she married my stepdad, Tom. I was born in 1976, in the closest town 'proper' to Fairbury: Pontiac,

Illinois. As soon as Mom was healthy enough to travel, we drove along country roads, highways, and interstates that connected one town to the next, across the country until we arrived in Phoenix, Arizona. My parents were able to rent a small, two-room shack across the street from the government projects on the corner of Van Buren and 20th Street. It housed a fold-out couch where my parents slept, and my three siblings and I scattered throughout on small pallets of blankets on the floor.

Mom frequently needed help with food and paying bills, and she knew from her Methodist upbringing that churches could help. She found the Church of Jesus, a small Pentecostal community, which was a mile up the road. Mom and Tom quickly gained support for the family in exchange for driving the church bus. When it was hot, we'd get popsicles to give to the kids as they got on the bus to go home. This was a win-win for us as kids because we got the leftover popsicles after everyone was dropped off Sunday afternoon.

My sisters, Pennie and Sis, connected with their Sunday school teacher, Aunt Darlene, in whom they found encouragement and a friend. The teacher for me and my brother, Pat, was Sister Wilma. She was a wide and squishy grandma who hugged every kid that came into her classroom. Whenever I saw her, she would wrap her jiggly arms around me, pulling me close to her heart. She'd say, "Joey, Jesus loves you so much, and I do too." Each time we got to church, in the morning or evening, I'd run off to find Sister Wilma because I knew a big hug was waiting for me. In that big, warm embrace, it felt like a safe haven as though all my worries had been washed away.

Church became a staple for the Hamack family; we'd be there anytime the church doors were open. Most Sunday evenings, there was food afterward, so it was a benefit for us to go as much as possible. We'd have to sit through two three-hour services where the choir would endlessly sing song after song about heaven, pearly gates, defeating the devil, and spending eternity with God. I had no idea what it meant, but they seemed to believe it with their entire being as the congregation clapped and swayed to the organ and upright bass the pastor played while he directed them. Then the Holy Ghost would 'come down,' and sister Pettigrew would run around the perimeter of the sanctuary, waving her hands and speaking in 'tongues' – which is the Holy Ghost's language. Once they finished, Pastor Outlaw (yes, that is his real name) would get up to deliver the message. This was true hellfire and brimstone preaching, with sweaty callouts of "Amen," "Well," and "Preach it" tossed back and forth between him and the congregation. When he'd really get going, he'd get into a high-pitched yell and spit, as he explained how we had to "let the Holy Ghost get in ya and receive all God's glory," igniting the organist's fingers and feet to accentuate his words as the congregation jumped to their feet and danced "In the Spirit." This small congregation felt like home to us. We became friends with the Outlaw's, Aunt Darlene, and Sister Wilma, who would remember my birthday for years after we moved away from Phoenix.

Although Mom's day job was as a nurse's aide, another life was always only a breath away for her and Tom. We were carnies. That's right, carnies. You may have seen us in a grocery store or church parking lot, maybe even at a county fair, throwing dimes at cheap glass, frying corn dogs, making caramel apples, running a kiddie ride, or just running around as unsupervised children. In our family, if you were old enough to count and have a small amount of responsibility, you worked at the carnival. It was a requirement to contribute to the family. My Mom worked the ticket booth, Tom worked a game, and my sisters babysat or worked in a food wagon. Since the carnival moved from town to town each week, we were fairly nomadic until all four of us kids had to go to school. Even then, whenever we were short on money, it was easy to find the carnival and head out. Whenever summer arrived or a long weekend approached, the Hamack family would pack up and be back on the road in a matter of hours.

The carnival life is like a family, with a strong hierarchy placing the big boss at the top. It has a bit of a mob-like feel; they certainly protect their own and follow a code. The code was simple. First, no cops; we handled problems within the family. Second, the big boss had the final say. And finally, respect and honor the family. A breach in any of these would not be tolerated. If you proved yourself, you would be accepted and have a place. Your reason for showing up to join didn't really matter. Some people were born into it, others were running away from something or someone. This brought all sorts of characters into the family. Some were married, with kids like us but most were single. There was easy access to drugs, sex, or whatever else you wanted, as long as you followed the Carnie Code.

As Mom, Tom, and our sister would head off to work, Pat and I were often left to fend for ourselves for most of the day. Mom would look in on us when she took a break and we'd stop by to say hello to Tom. Everyone in 'the show' knew who we were, so they were able to report where we were or when we were last seen. We would make the most of the time by visiting the vendor booths, trying free samples, watching rodeos and demolition derbies, looking for money that had fallen through the arena bleachers the night before, and stealing a few things along the way.

Patrick, Pat for short, was the feistiest of all of us. He had the temper of Kathy and Tom combined, cussed and smoked like a carnie, and will stand up for the most vulnerable. Yet, he was a complicated man with a well of emotions who would take two six-packs of beer and a 2 a.m. conversation to get to the heart of the matter.

He would say he was the black sheep of the family, which was funny because Pennie would say the same thing. I think Pat always won, though. If you tell him to go right, he'll go left. If you say jump, he'll sit down. I don't think it was him being resistant, but that he wanted to try to figure it out on his own. Pat was competitive in all things and will try to one-up you every time. He was a sports kid who loved soccer and Pele. He favored kung fu movies, was a master fort designer, could construct the steepest bike ramp, loved train sets, and could sing his heart out with me while we watched the Mickey Mouse Club, Star Search, or Kids Incorporated. He's thirteen months older than me. He was my overseer, best friend and hero.

We were no more than four and five years old when the summer adventures truly began. In the late 70s and early 80s, Skoal chewing tobacco had booths at county fairs, where they would introduce new flavors. We had no idea what it was, but several of the ride jocks used it and looked cool putting a wad in their cheeks. Pat and I were short enough that the vendors couldn't see our heads peeking over the tall display counters. We figured out how to snake one off the table, then ran to hide under the rodeo bleachers to see what all the fuss was all about. That small, round, green can wafted heavenly aromas when we opened it. A combination of mint and wet, woodsy earth drew both of us in to take an oversized wad and lodge it between our cheek and gums, just like the ride jocks. As the chew began to mix with my saliva, it was as if my body had turned on a faucet. Since I couldn't talk and hold it in my mouth at the same time, I had to swallow it. One full gulp of Skoal-flavored saliva and I was ruined for life; the way something smells is not always how it tastes. I quickly spat it out and told Pat it was gross. He may have kept it in for another few seconds – he IS the competitive one – then he spat it out as well. We threw the can in the trash and moved on to the next adventure under the bleachers, looking for money, sunglasses, and unopened candy.

When the show closed in one town, we packed up and headed to the next, picking up new characters to join the carnival. After the family said goodbye for the day, Pat and I would hang out behind the show to play and go see other kids whose parents were working as well. We loved to use the big semis as if they were giant jungle gyms, climbing all over and under them. Most semis had a small cabin ride jocks would use as living quarters. It was normal to see guys walking back to their trucks while on a break.

One guy had a small white dog that we'd stop and pet on occasion. He would always say hi and let us know we could always come by and pet the dog. One day, we were visiting as he was teaching his dog some tricks. He walked up to us and asked if we wanted to see them. Of course, we said yes, and he invited us to climb into his semi so he could show us. As we got in, he closed the curtains to cover the windshield and started playing with the dog. While he was doing that, he unzipped his pants to expose himself. At the time, we didn't know what that guy was doing was wrong; nobody ever talked to us about something like that. We thought he was a nice guy and that he wanted to show us his cool dog tricks, but instead, he was some horrible man who thought it was okay to prey on two little boys.

A few days later, Pat and I were in the bathroom, and that same guy walked in. He said hi to us and started to ask if we wanted to come back to his truck again that afternoon. Luckily, Tom had walked in as well and overheard what he said. Tom stepped all the way up to his face, his nose touching the guy's cheek.

"If you ever come around my boys again, I will fucking kill you," he said.

He stood there staring at the guy, his entire body charged with all the anger he had repressed for decades as he waited for the guy to walk out. Tom turned and commanded us to get back to the trailer, where we spent the rest of the evening. I was scared we'd get spanked when Mom came to check on us a few hours later, but she didn't say anything. She made sure we had eaten and ready for bed, then left for the night. That was the last day we ever saw that man; he had violated the Carnie Code and nobody spoke of it afterward.

Tom Hamack was a six-foot-one, Irish, reddish-brown-haired man with a mustache. His face was speckled with freckles and weathered from smoking his entire life. He had horrible hygiene habits and only two teeth in which he held an ever-burning cigarette. He was born in Tucson, AZ, where he was raised by his aunt, Agnes, soon after both of his parents died.

While serving in Vietnam, Tom was exposed, like so many other soldiers to Agent Orange, which caused several physical and mental health issues. As an adult, he carried the heavy weight of the war and losing his parents, which showed up in his earth-shattering bouts of anger. This was ultimately his Achilles heel, and he was dishonorably discharged after punching his commanding officer. After being released from the military, he resolved not to let his anger get the best of him again.

He went on to graduate from Grand Canyon University with a doctorate in Biblical Theology, although one would never know that as he rarely shared it. Tom had a voracious appetite for reading, mostly war novels, Bible commentary, or the local newspaper. Never finding a comfortable space in regular society, he joined a traveling carnival and found a community of misfits that he could relate to. This is where he'd ultimately meet my mom.

There was always something a little off about Tom. He had a hard time being in social environments; it seemed he couldn't relate or connect with people. That became more apparent as I transitioned into adulthood. We believe he would now be diagnosed with Asperger's.

I called Tom "Dad" for most of my life. However, we're not certain he is, and I've lived most of my life as if he wasn't.

One day, we arrived in a town that didn't allow camping behind the carnival, so, as we often did, we made camp at the local KOA down the road. Here, we lived in a combination of a large green canvas army tent for the kids and a small travel trailer that Mom towed with her green and brown-paneled station wagon. As 'the show' was getting ready to open, Mom had brought us over from the KOA site while she finished setting up. The show was nestled in a narrow downtown, where they had blocked off streets for games, rides, and food wagons to line the square. Mom instructed us to stay close by as she finished up, then we headed back to the KOA where Pat and I would stay on our own for the evening. We immediately forgot what she said, ran off to explore the new wonderland, and lost track of time. Our adventures had taken us away from reality. Four and five years old aren't great timekeepers.

When we returned, we couldn't find Mom or our huge station wagon. Pat and I knew we were in big trouble for wandering too far and not being there when Mom was ready to leave. We had failed to "listen and be good"! We asked some of the crew members who worked for her where she was, but they all said she had left. Pat and I looked at each other, knowing what would happen if we disobeyed her rules. Then we decided it would be best to walk back to the KOA ourselves. With a childlike treasure map to our destination in his head, Pat grabbed my hand and we were off. Straight ahead, turn here, then up another block, turn there and we were at the main artery of the local highway. We walked up the exit ramp and headed in what we thought was the right direction; home. Cars whizzed by as if pushed by a brewing storm, throwing trash up and down the side of the highway, along with a sign that we were on the right path. Then a dollar bill blew right up to my feet. As I was picking up my treasure, a police car pulled up. When the officer asked where we were going, we told him the story of our search for our home just up the road. Not quite understanding where we were going, he put us in the back of the car and drove us to where we had started. When we arrived, there was a frenzy of people looking for us.

Mom was a mess and yelled, "Where the hell have you been?"

She said she'd had to run an errand for her boss and that's why the car was gone. Mom spent the next few minutes explaining what happened to clear up any concern she had abandoned us. When the cop felt comfortable this was just a mishap, he excused us and waved goodbye. She thanked him and loaded us up to go back to the KOA.

When we got there, the big boss was there with some other people who had all joined the search for the lost boys. He was pissed! Already flushed from too many glasses of scotch, he resembled a pirate captain furious with his crew. We had brought the cops to 'the show' and delayed the opening, causing him to lose some booty he wanted to add to his own treasure chest. We were sure that walking the plank was the only solution, but he had other ideas. As punishment, Mom allowed him to spank us. Our bare bottoms were swollen with hand welts, matching the color of the big boss's face. Tears ran down our dirt-covered cheeks, revealing the toll of that day's adventure. It was a reminder that even little kids have to follow the Carnie Code; no cops. Listen and be good.

After Pat and Joey's excellent adventure, we couldn't be left alone anymore, and Mom had to find a sitter for us whenever the camp was too far away from the showground. The next town required just that, and Mom found a local to babysit us. Now, babysitting for carnie kids didn't require any skills or certification. Just a "yes" and you could make a little cash.

The following afternoon, Mom pulled into a trailer park and up to a weathered, brown mobile home. A thin, wavy-haired woman appeared at the door to greet us and show us where we could play. We settled into the corner of the living room while she went about her business.

Throughout the day, many people knocked on the door, came in, and walked down the hall. At the beginning of the second day, we settled in to playing and watching the people come in and out of the house again. Late afternoon, when we had just finished lunch, another knock rattled on the door. However, it was different this time. It was thunderous and startled everyone in the trailer. As the woman peered out the window, someone yelled, "SHIT!!!" Immediately, the cops burst through the door with guns to arrest our babysitter on drug charges.

In the back of a cop's car for the second time in a week, I feared what would happen to me and Pat for breaking the Carnie Code. Mom had to explain why her children were with a drug dealer. We brought too much attention to the carnival and put everyone in danger. The carnival boss couldn't take the risk of it happening again, so we packed up the station wagon, hitched up the trailer, and headed back to Phoenix.

Turkeys and deserts

We quickly settled into the cadence of life back in Phoenix, reconnected with the Church of Jesus and found space in the trailer park where Mom's best friend, Nonnie, lived. Her kids were about the same age as my sisters, so we had built-in community and much-needed babysitting. We lived in a small white-and-green-striped trailer where Mom and Tom occupied the front bed, which converted back and forth to the dining room table. Pennie and Sis slept in the back of the trailer with me and Pat. Their beds were top bunks that converted from cabinets to beds by folding down the openings to make long, narrow twin beds on each side. Finally, we, the boys, slept in the bottom bunks below our sisters. The trailer was also home to a perpetually pregnant cat and a dog named Shaggy.

Nonnie would remain my babysitter while the other children went to school, until it was finally my turn. Each morning, my sisters would make sure we were dressed for the day and would then drop me off at Nonnie's house on their way to school. With everyone off to school and Nonnie back in bed, I'd get bored pretty quickly. I could play with the few toys Nonnie had or explore parts of her trailer. The bathroom mirror was a perfect place to make funny faces, act silly, and even give myself a haircut the day before school pictures. After a few hours of playing, I would walk down the main driveway of the trailer park to catch the bus to half-day kindergarten.

At school, I had the best teacher who would always make sure I was a priority. She was kind, funny, loved to sing songs, and took special care of me. She would always ask me how my day was and encourage me to play with the other children. Her care reminded me of Sister Wilma's hugs and attention in Sunday school. Learning the alphabet was one of the most exciting parts of the day. Each letter was a blow-up cartoon with its assigned letter across its chest. I remember Mr. M in particular because we were introduced to him on the same day my desk neighbor, Renee, said she saw her parents kissing and asked if I wanted her to kiss me. As our lips touched, our teacher saw us out of the corner of her eye. We had to sit there listening to her explain why kissing wasn't something that should be done in school and that if it happened again, she would have to tell our parents.

When the school year was nearing the end, Mom and Tom made plans to work the carnival for the summer. They got an early notice to meet the carnival in a nearby town, and Mom went to the school to get the rest of our schoolwork for the last few weeks. We'd finish our work on the road and then mail it back to school. But there was no notice for us kids. One day, we were in school and the next day, we were packing to leave. No goodbyes to friends, teachers, or my first kiss. The Hamack's were off on another adventure through New Mexico to the Dakotas.

At the end of the summer, Tom's Aunt Agnes became ill. Instead of returning to Phoenix, we went to her house in Tucson, Arizona. Tom was raised by Agnes, whom we called

Nana. Even as an adult, there are two distinctive things I remember about her. One, she always had Smucker's apricot preserves; and two, she was a fiery old Irish woman who could pinch you so hard that your soul would scream. She favored Patrick over the rest of us and paid little attention to my sisters; probably because they were not Tom's children. Tucson was a newfound wonderland that was perfect for two little boys with open desert, long summers, Eegee's, and friends who lived on every block, no matter which way our bikes or feet took us.

When we weren't riding our bikes or building forts, we were in the huge alley behind Nana's house. It was bigger than most alleys because it was the point where three different streets converged; it had a baseball diamond-shaped space where all the neighborhood kids played. Pat knew how to rally the entire neighborhood by coordinating hide-and-seek, dirt-clod fights, and even shot-and-run – where he would fire an arrow with his bow into the sky while we all just stood there and watched it disappear as if it left the stratosphere. It was always an adventure when Pat was around.

When Nana moved into an assisted living center, the Hamacks settled into her house, where we would live for the next few years. Mom went back to her job as a nurse's aide, working the night shift. In addition to this work, she would handle private cases in people's homes, typically end-of-life care. This type of work was easy to come by and helped make ends meet since she was paid under the table and didn't have to wait for a paycheck. Tom found a job at the

Tucson Electric Company until he was burned in a chemical fire. After the incident, he was home for weeks, and when he recovered and tried to go back to work, he just couldn't. He eventually transitioned to various entry-level jobs. We'd come home from school to be welcomed by him regularly. Given Tom's demeanor and social awkwardness, you didn't get much further in conversation with him than the usual pleasantries. He was more comforting than Mom though. Occasionally, on Sunday evenings, we'd settle in to watch The Wonderful World of Disney. I would scoot in beside him, then he would awkwardly bring his arm around me and pull me in closer. My little heart would beat fast for a moment, then slow. My breathing would get in sync with his and my arm would rise and fall as his belly filled and emptied. There didn't need to be any words, Tom didn't have any and wasn't used to saying, "I love you." Just a moment of closeness was enough to give my soul a few drops of nourishment.

Even without rent or a mortgage, it was difficult for my parents to pay the bills, and that made us regular recipients of food boxes. Mom researched the schedule of which churches were distributing boxes, where to get government commodities, and planned the early morning treks across sleepy Tucson to get in line. This was part of the weekly activities, along with early morning yard sales. We stood in what seemed to be the worst line at Disneyland to get boxes filled with monochromatic items printed in black san serif capital letters. They contained a giant aluminum can of peanut butter that required a large wooden spoon to mix the separated oil and peanuts, white bread, puffed wheat or rice cereal, powdered milk, honey or sugar, whole chicken, and a block of cheese, though it wasn't quite cheese or quite Velveeta. These were the staples of our home. Mom did her best to make the milk go further by splitting the gallon of whole milk in half and replacing the second half with a half-gallon of powdered milk. It always had that slight powdery flavor that was a little off, so we'd just add more sugar to our cereal to cover it up. My friend, Tiffany, and her family also received government food. But since her mom had special dietary needs, they got a lot of dried fruit and juices, which seemed weird to little kids. None of us liked the prunes, dried fruit, or juice. Pat and I rarely complained about the food, at least not within earshot of Mom. If she did hear us, we would be sent to bed without a meal and be called "an ungrateful, snot nosed brat."

I learned to fear and respect Mom at an early age. If something wasn't done the way she wanted it, or if we got in trouble for any of a myriad of reasons, we would have battle scars to remind us for a week. We were on heightened alert when she was on the warpath because we didn't know how she was going to respond, and she knew how to inflict pain. If we didn't listen, she could snatch your earlobe and twist it until you fell to the ground. When approached from behind, she'd grab your hair, pulling you to the floor where she would be in a better position to spank you. A belt wasn't needed though, as the nearest shoe, strap, tree branch, or her bare hand would do the job well to bring us to order. If we moved, we got it worse; if she missed, we got it more and harder; and if we fell, we had to take it on the floor while she stood over us, all the while berating us into an empty shell, now numb, waiting for it to end. Pat took the brunt of the beatings, mostly because he wouldn't stand still and was stubborn enough not to give in and shed a tear. The spankings would end on the floor as Mom whipped him, leaving outlined welts wherever they landed on his small frame as she screamed at him in a rage. Most of the time, Pat would just take it, and when he made it to our bedroom, he'd let out the emotions of everything that had just happened. With his body shaking from the pain and heaviness in his heart, he would lie on his bed, his fuzzy red, white and black checkered blanket wrapped tightly around his body, comforting his soul. He wouldn't say anything. Instead, he'd just lay there and cry, letting his blanket hold him. I would sit on the side of his bed and ask if he was okay; he would only nod and pull the blanket closer to his face, curled up into a fetal position and close his eyes. Then I would sit there for a minute and then slowly get up and go to my bed and play quietly or rest. After seeing what Mom would do if we didn't follow the rules, I committed to memorizing or checking off a list of what she told us to do to make sure we didn't get in trouble. The few spankings I received on the floor, with her hands or belt becoming the weapon of choice – hitting my arms, back, and legs – were enough to teach me to follow the rules; "listen, and be good."

The spanking, berating, and hitting wasn't isolated with the kids though. During the day, our house was pretty quiet, even with four kids running around. Tom was in charge of making sure meals were cooked, chores done, and rooms cleaned while Mom slept. If we got too loud, we'd hear her yell from her bedroom, "You better shut up or I'm coming out there." Pat and I were in the living room and he had done something to upset Tom, so Tom started yelling at him. Not long after Tom yelled, we heard the bedroom door open. Mom came out in a long nightgown with curlers in her hair. She quickly stomped down the hallway yelling, "I told you to fucking shut up. What the hell is wrong with you? You stupid son of a bitch! I have to work tonight." She began slapping him; first, in the chest as he towered over her a good ten inches, then with all her might, she pushed him backwards. He fell over the coffee table, broke off one of the legs and landed halfway on the couch. She continued screaming and slapping for a few moments, then got up from him and returned to her bedroom, screaming obscenities as she walked down the hall. Tom laid there for a moment, stunned but not overly surprised. Then he collected himself and began to clean up the mess. He didn't say another word to any of us. I stood there, shocked at what I'd just seen. A man who clearly could have knocked Mom down screamed louder or possibly even hurt her just took it. The promise he'd made to himself when he was discharged from the military to never hit anyone again took precedence. Pat and I silently got up, gathered our things, and went to our rooms to play quietly for the rest of the evening.

Tom didn't do much with me and Pat, unless Mom had told him to. He would occasionally take us to the zoo or the park to fish in the local pond or watch the turtles swim around. The Davis-Monthan Air Show was a highlight for Tom. He knew all the planes, how fast they could go, and when they were used in history. He was like an encyclopedia of military aircrafts, sharing as many facts and statistics as he could. It was nice to see Tom come alive and engage with us. It even inspired Pat to try building model airplanes. Tom would tell stories about the plane while Pat put it together. I was the extra hand pushing pieces out of the plastic mold. It was a rare moment when the Hamack men sat around a table and shared an experience in which we were all fully involved, which I was also a part of.

Mom also began looking for a new church. Since Church of Jesus in Phoenix had made such a strong impression on us, we needed to find something similar in this new city. We quickly found Eastside Assemblies of God, which was within walking distance of our home. They were not as charismatic as our previous church, but that was okay because they had a lot of programs for families and children. We fit in quickly and became friends with several families. Pat and I befriended some of the pastor's sons, and my sisters befriended other girls in the youth group. The church became another refuge for us. Life at home was difficult, but church felt like a space of normalcy. Adults made eye contact with us, knew our names, gave us hugs, and were genuinely happy to see us. It was refreshing to be encouraged and sometimes celebrated for memorizing Bible verses, bringing friends, or even putting a half-full barrel of pennies into my missionary piggy bank. I looked forward to every opportunity to be at church, as a sense of belonging came so easily there and for the fact that we were given lots of candy...just to keep it real. Tom connected with Pastor Ed because they both had a love for studying the Bible and a deep understanding of theology. For someone who stood out in most situations, Tom seemed to settle into a cadence like he did at Church of Jesus. He was a dedicated helper; ushering, doing manual labor, driving the bus, or whatever the church needed.

Tom met some dads who helped with the Royal Rangers, our Christian scout troop. This gave him a space to be a little more himself and to relate to some guys who had also served in Vietnam. They helped him adjust to family-church life, and he could talk about what was going on inside. These newfound friendships and theological conversations with Pastor Ed drew Tom back to his love for studying the Scriptures. He had a stack of books, his Bible, commentaries, and a notebook on the end table next to his chair in the living room. He'd sit there for hours, absorbed in reading, writing, and smoking a pipe that he kept in a red container on the same end table. I loved the sweet, woodsy aroma of the tobacco as he puffed slowly, holding the pipe in his mouth with his two remaining teeth. Tom never seemed to mind that he didn't have more teeth, although he always had a large Irish red mustache growing over his upper lip, possibly to hide his lack of pearly whites.

When the days would grow shorter and the sun began to set lower over the mountains west of Tucson, a chill filled the desert air, welcoming late fall and early winter to the dusty city. Thanksgiving kicked us into a celebratory mode that we didn't experience too often. Food banks and churches were more generous, and Mom knew how to take advantage of several items that were added to our cupboards. The first holiday meal had all the staples; green bean casserole, marshmallow sweet potatoes, mashed potatoes, rolls, cranberry jelly, and the coveted relish tray my brother and I made. The feast didn't begin until mid-afternoon, and the Macy's Day Parade kept us busy with its balloons, marching bands, floats, and the occasional star doing a bad rendition of a Christmas song. When the parade ended, we knew the meal was close to being ready and we could now begin to eat the relish tray we had worked so hard to create, piled with olives, pickles, and carrots in perfect form on 1950s glass platters. When the golden-brown turkey came out of the oven, Tom carved it; we'd all sit down, say what we were thankful for, and feast. Most of the time, meals were simple and sparse, so this was truly an extravagant experience for us; one to be savored. We'd wait an hour or so before jumping into dessert with pies, ambrosia, Cool Whip, and cakes. By the time a football game started in the late afternoon, our bellies had bulged beyond our waistbands in pure bliss. In our house, nothing went to waste, so half the leftovers were frozen and the rest became turkey and stuffing in a thousand different ways for weeks to come. Even the carcass went into a pot and mixed with egg noodles for Sunday dinner.

The holidays would bring a rare warmth to our home with a month-long celebration of giving thanks and decorating the tree. The Douglas fir would be adorned with school-made ornaments and bulbs. Just before adding the star, we'd wrap individually strung cranberry and popcorn garlands in fake tinsel, which our cat ate and vomited back up several times during the season. Although Mom was far from Julia Child, she had a way with holiday treats like fudge, candy, and cookies. She'd spend an entire weekend in the kitchen over the stove, slowly stirring the sweetened condensed milk into the rest of the mixture before pouring it onto a baking sheet. With Bing Crosby Holiday Classics humming on the record player in the background, Mom sang as she moved around the kitchen, taking cookies in and out of the oven, melting chocolate for candy, and waiting for the fudge to set. The stern, authoritative woman we were so used to faded into the background, revealing a warm-hearted mother tethered to another moment in time. She seemed happy, lighter, and her words softened, allowing us to enjoy time as a family.

With the holidays in full swing, it would become time for the Christmas pageant and cantata. Pat and I would always be part of the children's Christmas show. When you reached fifth grade, you could audition for supporting roles, then sixth grade for leading roles. Fifth grade allowed me to show my talent, and I got a part as one of the X's in a musical about the culture trying to take Christ out of Christmas and replace it with Xmas. It was way ahead of its time in the 80's and really dealt with consumerism and moving away from traditional values of giving thanks for what we had. Sixth grade allowed my inner thespian to really shine as Good King Wenceslas. The costume was spectacular; a purple tunic, a matching cape trimmed with fake fur, a perfectly fitted crown, and gold shoes. I acted and sang as if I were the center of a Broadway show. Mom sat in the second row from the front, which was her usual spot, ready to watch us perform. Occasionally, I'd look out into the audience to see the lights reflecting off her big glasses and catch a broad smile as she watched proudly. On the Sunday before Christmas, the cantata celebrated the birth of Christ with a floor-to-ceiling Christmas tree that doubled as a riser for the choir. Mom lit up, singing along to the songs she knew and humming along to the ones she didn't.

There is some nostalgia in these traditions, garnished with the usual dysfunctional family squabbles, the dog eating something off the table, the cat getting stuck in the Christmas tree, and the kids peeking at presents while the parents were away. Though there were a few gifts, there was a sense of warmth and connection to one another that served as a gift we would build on as adults. For the longest time, this was all the family life I knew.

Family life

39

I walked into my Sunday school classroom and sat down at the back, away from the other children. Another kid, whom I hadn't seen before, came in and sat down next to me. Our Sunday school teachers, Mr. and Mrs. Graham, were walking around saying hello to everyone when Mr. Graham approached the two of us. He already knew my name, but the boy was new.

"Hello, I'm Mr. Graham. What's your name?" he asked.

The boy smiled and said his name was Matt. Mr. Graham greeted him and introduced him to me. When the teacher left, Matt and I awkwardly tried to continue the conversation. It took a few minutes to warm up to each other but then he turned out to be a lot of fun. As Sunday school finished up, we transitioned to Children's Church in the big auditorium and decided to sit next to each other.

Matt and I quickly became inseparable at church. Even though we had different interests, we clicked and enjoyed hanging out together. He loved to talk about sports, and I pretended to know what he was talking about. Matt lived about a mile north of me, so we didn't go to the same school. I'd occasionally see him at Royal Rangers, but he'd go to practice or games instead. So, church was the place where we'd see each other regularly. When we did see each other, we'd talk about our week and try to make plans for me to go to his house after church.

Before we went over to Matt's house, we'd go out to eat. I didn't have much experience eating in restaurants, so I was nervous when they handed me the menu. Matt's dad, Dennis, asked me what I wanted to eat.

I looked at Matt, who said, "A hot dog with everything on it." So, I ordered the same thing, but no onions.

Dennis replied, "You can have it any way you want it, Joey."

The restaurant was a peculiar place. I had always been told what to eat when we went anywhere. My family was on a tight budget so Mom would order for all the kids and we only drank water, no soda. Now, I was offered a menu and could choose anything I wanted – a hot dog, hamburger, meatloaf, you name it. I enjoyed every bite of the hot dog and fries the waitress put in front of me. When we got back to Matt's house, it was time to explore the neighborhood, play in the backyard with his dog, Honeybee, and the G.I. Joe's in his bedroom, or go to the racket club for a swim.

While my family went to church every Sunday, Matt's family was a little less concerned about church and more focused on spending time together. They regularly went hiking or camping in the Tucson Mountains. Matt's mom, Leann, would call my mom and ask if I could go with them for the weekend so we could go on hikes that took us to a watering hole where we could swim. Matt's parents encouraged him to explore, so he'd run off with me close behind. We'd climb rocks, look for lizards, and find uniquely shaped rocks to run back and show to his mom so she could name them. In the evenings, we would sit around the campfire, eat dinner, and then go to bed. Once settled into our tent, we'd talk about our adventures until one of us fell asleep.

Dennis was a doctor and sometimes we'd go to the office with him for the day, which gave us a whole new landscape to explore. We horsed around in the hearing test booth, watched TV in the break room, and checked in with his dad between patients. It was on one of these trips that I experienced Taco Bell for the first time. When his dad asked what I wanted in my tacos, I told him "a soft taco and mild sauce." He asked if I wanted two. That's when my mind exploded. I had never been offered more food before and didn't know how to react, so I asked if it wouldn't be too much.

He smiled and said, "I'll take care of it. And no onions, right?"

I smiled and nodded in amazement that he remembered something so small.

Even though I moved frequently and stopped going to Eastside Assembly, Matt and I stayed connected by talking on the phone. It was rare that we saw one another, though I loved being around his family; they were genuinely interested in me. Dennis would greet me when he came home from work and Leann put her hand on my shoulder when she spoke with me. They asked me questions about school, what my interests were, and encouraged me to think about what I wanted to be when I grew up. There wasn't anything in particular that made it special; it was simply that adults were showing genuine interest in me. It was in stark contrast to my home life and at times felt like I was in a world. At Matt's house, I was just a kid playing G.I Joe's with his friend, running around in the backyard with his dog or sitting on the couch watching a movie. In moments like that, I wished I was part of this family instead of my own. I felt at ease there, with nobody yelling. I was comforted and safe.

In fourth grade, Mom and Tom joined a group called Marriage Encounter. Couples would go to a hotel for a weekend to work on their relationship. Pat and I spent the weekend with some family friends, and when it was time to be reunited with our parents, we headed off to a hotel just off the freeway. We walked into a hotel ballroom where other kids were waiting and positioned in front of a movable wall that separated the two rooms. As it opened, the adults were singing a song they had learned. As my eyes scanned the newly visible adults, I skipped over mine twice. I wasn't used to seeing them holding hands, standing close together, and smiling. Then kids ran to their parents and talked about their weekend experience with whomever they had been with for a few days. We had a quick exchange, then left the weekend with a bumper sticker for the car and a candle to burn regularly as a symbol of their love and to never let it go out. This was supposed to be a solution to the constant nuclear explosions they had been having lately. It seemed to work for a short time; they would connect with other couples to talk for a while. There was one monthly family activity this inspired; you would secretly drop off donuts to another family so they knew someone was thinking of them. We all piled into the car; Mom stopped to buy a dozen donuts and we drove across Tucson to drop them off at a stranger's house. We sat in the backseat as Mom went into the donut shop and reemerged with two boxes; one for the unsuspecting family and a half dozen for us. The boxes sat securely on our laps as we made our way to the house. I thought about how delicious mine would be when we finished the delivery. The powdered sugar, jelly-filled, fluffy cloud would ooze as I bit into it, leaving a white outline on my lips. Yes, the children who received the surprise of these delicious treats would bask in a quick dose of sugar.

By the middle of fourth grade, it turned out that Marriage Encounter hadn't helped Mom and Tom enough to stay together. Mom relented and said they couldn't be around each other anymore. It was a big change in our home. Since working at the carnival had been part of how they made ends meet for the past few years, Tom had connections with some shows that could help him get a job. So, Mom bought him a bus ticket and dropped him off at the station. Afterwards, Mom gave a simple explanation that they were no longer going to be married. There were no goodbyes, no hugs, no last chance to sit next to Tom and snuggle in close to watch TV. The candle had been blown out; the random donut deliveries ceased. It was now only Mom and the kids regularly at odds with one another. Our buffer was off to the carnival to begin his own life. This left the responsibility of caring for the children and Pennie would be responsible for filling both parent roles now.

Pennie Louise is the oldest of our four siblings. To make sure everyone knew how to spell her first name, she would say, "It's not Penny with a Y. It's P.E.N.N.I.E. Not like the coin." She is kind, tender-hearted, quick-witted, a jokester, and a creative writer. She collects carousel horse figurines, is a master fisherman, laughs with her whole body, and can barely catch her breath when she gets going. To this day, she is the only one to still call me Joey or Bubba. Pennie is seven years older than me, and she is a half-sister with the same mom. She is the maternal one of the siblings, mostly out of necessity because mom wasn't around much.

Pennie and Sis had a lot more to say about the divorce and Tom. It quickly came out that he had sexually abused them and wasn't a good guy anyway. As a nine-year-old, I still found it difficult to process what that even meant, but I could at least see the pain in their eyes and understand that it was extremely bad. Even though Mom never mentioned the abuse, she regularly berated Tom as if he was now the enemy and should be treated as such. She continued to call him a "son of a bitch" or a "piece of shit," even when she dropped us off to spend time with him.

As Mom started working more often overnight, my sisters would step in even more to take care of the house and the kids. She found ways for us to get to church and participate as much as we could. We'd attend regular Sunday and Wednesday services, youth groups for my sisters, Royal Rangers, and Jr. Bible Quiz for me. The church always stepped in to support us. I looked forward to going to the church gym every Tuesday night. I had proudly donned my oversized khaki pants and shirt, wore my red Ranger bandana, and pinned on all my Buckaroo badges. Friends and leaders were waiting to greet the Hamack boys, inviting us to play pool, basketball, or work up a sweat running around in a game of tag. As Mom and Tom moved toward divorce, the leaders, William and Craft, spent extra time with me and Pat. They had become friends with Tom and missed having him around. What's more was that they actually saw the sadness in our eyes and gave us extra pats on the back. These men showed me that I can do hard things if I put in the work, and that not everything will turn out the way you expect. That's why low-stakes practice is so important. If a leader saw me struggling, they would encourage me to try again. If I didn't get it, they would hold me accountable and challenge me to work on it at home and then come back the next week and try again. It built resilience along with the knowledge that I could actually do the hard stuff if I worked at it.

Pat and I handled the divorce differently. Even though Tom hadn't interacted with us much, he had been the buffer between us and Mom, and his absence made it clear that we had to figure out how to fit into the strict rules that Mom was now directly enforcing. I knew how to make myself smaller and less present in the room to avoid Mom's wrath. I could "listen, and be good," without being seen. Pat went in the opposite direction by getting into fights, arguing, and stealing things. And even though I tried to keep my head low, his adventures did get me in trouble as well.

Pat had a thing for bicycles; whenever we were in a store, he'd go straight to the magazine rack to find the one with BMX bikes splashed across the cover. He had a friend who actually got the magazine at his house and he would borrow it to bring home, flip through it over and over, and then talk about the design and the riders. One day, after school, he brought home a bike. It was a rad BMX with rear pegs and handbrakes, which was the coveted bike for every cool kid in the '80s. When I asked him where he got the bike, he said he found it in the alley. I took him at his word until the following week when he was sick and I rode that bike to school. I was sooo cool, riding past the other kids on my brother's BMX. I had arrived! Well, until the next day when I was called to the principal's office before I could do some sweet jumps. When I got there, I found my mom and Pat were waiting for me. Pat had actually stolen the bike, and the owner had seen me riding it to school the day before. Mom was furious. Even though I wasn't the culprit, we had embarrassed Mom and had gotten the police involved. We'd broken the Carnie Code, as well as Mom's own precept. We accepted an all too familiar beating and berating, we were grounded to our rooms for a month and had to wash baseboards and walls on weekends. In all of these, that didn't faze Pat. Within a few weeks, he was caught shoplifting gum from the grocery store and was in real trouble. Mom had to pick him up at the police station. The officer told him the next step would be juvenile detention; that must have scared him enough that at least he didn't get caught.

Summers required a bit of coordination for me and Pat. We needed structure to keep us occupied, with Pat's new adventures and run-ins with the cops. Churches had begun holding week-long events called Vacation Bible School, so Mom signed us up at several churches throughout June. It would be full of activities like singing, teaching, snacks, more singing, crafts, and a finale where we'd show all our parents what we'd learned about Jesus. This was my chance to show off my singing and drama skills – which never failed to make me feel seen and appreciated. Whenever the opportunity came to sing a solo or a song by myself, I jumped at the chance. I'd sing ad nauseam whilst Pat kept telling me to shut up. For the finale, I put on my best suit – which made me totally overdressed for the occasion – combed my hair, and practiced in the mirror for the final prep. Then it was showtime! When it was my turn, I didn't go to the side of the stage where the other kids stood during their performances. I grabbed the microphone from the stand and walked down the stairs to the main floor. Knowing the following day we would be back in our home, away from the encouraging leaders, missing the hugs and smiles, I began singing "I Am a Promise, I Am a Possibility" with every ounce of enthusiasm I could muster. Almost willing it into existence, it was my dream, my hope that I was something more than what Mom said I was, than a kid with divorced parents, I had the possibility to be more than that. When I finished, I got a standing ovation. Actually, it was just the usual clapping from parents who were tired from the week and anxious for this silly thing to be over. I struggled to fit into the social norms of sports and academics at school. This was the one place where I felt I could be myself, a place where I belonged. My mom, my VBS teacher, and a few other parents praised me for an amazing performance. I beamed at the praise and couldn't wait for the next chance to show off my theatrical skills.

The cycle of a school year, then summer, became a way of measuring where I was on the timeline of life. That and Nana's house were the two grounding points of my existence. When fifth grade started, Nana died and her house was sold to pay for medical bills and her funeral. Mom couldn't afford to buy the house, and that set us on a path of moving from small apartments to old trailers, studio apartments, and then back again for the next four years. As part of Mom's morning trip to the grocery store to buy discounted meat for dinner, she would meander through the store, picking up empty boxes. The car would be overflowing with empty boxes from canned vegetables and fresh fruit, ready to be unloaded and packed.

Once Mom found an affordable apartment, we loaded our blue 1970s Cadillac with as much as we could, turning and flipping boxes to fit next to each other like a game of Tetris. With furniture tied to the roof and hanging out of the trunk, Mom drove slowly down the street, making sure nothing fell off. When we arrived at our new apartment, it was a race to unload and then back to the house to pack again. We kept moving back and forth for about three times until the house was empty. And there it was, my elementary school memories sitting in the empty house. A movie reel played highlights of building forts with couch cushions and a makeshift boxing ring in the living room where Pat gave me my first black eye. My bedroom, where we'd played with friends under piles of stuffed animals. The hallway, where we tossed the ball with my pet hamster. The backyard, where Pat had taught me to ride a bike next to our rabbit cage. Then there was the Palo Verde tree that held a tire swing where Pat and I would push each other, which doubled as a rock sling where I paid him back for the black eye. All those memories echoed through the empty rooms now, whispering goodbye and fading to black.

Our new apartment would take us to a new part of town on the southeast side of Tucson. Sis, Pat, and I shared a bedroom, while Mom and Pennie shared the master bedroom. Each of us started new schools; Sis at a new high school, Pat and I at a new elementary school, and Pennie at a small Christian school on the northside of town. Life was different now and we had to make new friends in the neighborhood and at school. It was there that I met Mr. Johnson, my fifth-grade teacher.

Mr. Johnson loved two things; science and music. He made science come alive with experiments and tests to see if what the textbook said was true. We spent weeks on the light part of science as he discussed prisms and something new he was reading about called fiber optics. He challenged us to be curious and to also try new things. When our class needed a new student council member, he asked me to be one of two fifth grade representatives. I knew it was a job for cool kids, and nervously aware that I was far from being one of them, I joined with trepidation. He kept encouraging me to find my place among the other kids. To my surprise, the other students welcomed me as I was.

Mr. Johnson was a man of many talents; he conducted the school choir and directed the musical, Oliver Twist, that year. When the auditions were announced, I knew I wanted the lead. The audition was pretty casual. I just went to class early and he had me sing "America The Beautiful." To my surprise, I got the lead!

We practiced for weeks to get all the scenes down with twenty-five other kids and a couple of other leads. Opening night was full of excitement and nerves, but it went well. Everyone remembered their lines and cues, except for a little wardrobe malfunction where I couldn't get my pants on during a costume change; it was a hit. All my friends called me Oliver for the rest of the school year.

It was moments like these – Mr. Johnson encouraging me to try something new like student council, Matt's family inviting me to spend time with them, and attention from the men from our Royal Ranger group – that gave me hope that someone cared. Instead of robbing me of a childhood, these people worked to give me a sense of normalcy in my chaotic home life.

Peach fuzz

53

Because of our carnie experience, we'd often get visited by friends from the carnival who stopped by to say hello to Mom and Tom. After the divorce, however, Mom would bring home men she met while out that night. She would sneak them out early in the morning, trying not to wake us. We knew someone was in Mom's room, though, because Pennie was either in bed with Sis or there were blankets on the couch in the living room.

When Pennie began to show interest in a boy, she brought him to the apartment a few times. As Mom was introduced to him, she acted weird and was more friendly than usual. A few weeks later, I came home from school to find Pennie upset; she had been crying but wouldn't talk about it. She only alluded to Mom doing something with the guy she liked. Pennie had already been tired of the random men she was being kicked out of her bed for, but now Mom had crossed the line with her friend. Pennie had stayed in touch with Aunt Darlene in Phoenix and told her what was going on. A long weekend was approaching and Aunt Darlene asked if Pennie could come to Phoenix to get away. At the end of the weekend, Mom sat Pat and I down and explained to us that Pennie was going to stay in Phoenix and wouldn't be coming home. Once again, there were no hugs, no goodbyes, it was just a matter of fact as Mom explained she had gone to live with Aunt Darlene. She wasn't just the buffer for Mom, but the one to hold me when I was scared, coordinated games and fun activities while Mom was out of the house, made us laugh, and hugged me before bed. My big sister, the person who took care of me, was gone. Pat and I were losing another layer of separation from Mom and would begin to see more of who she was.

It seemed that our front and back doors were constantly opening and closing with a stream of men. Mom would meet a lot of these guys at the Post Time Pub, a local bar on the southwest side of Tucson. It was western-themed, with a dance floor where Mom would take us once or twice a month, now that our sisters were away from home. We could get Shirley Temple's and sit in a booth while she flirted with a guy. Occasionally, we'd have to do the two-step until either a guy came along, or we'd stepped on her feet so much that she'd get pissed off and give up. When she did meet a guy, we would sit and wait for her. Mom wouldn't bring him home right away, instead, she'd take us home and then go back to meet him. Either way, each guy was stranger than the one before.

Our first candidate for a new stepdad was Marcus, a curly-haired, skinny man who always had a funny smell about him. I don't think he worked because he was always home in the middle of the day. He became a bit of a babysitter for us boys while Mom worked. We would always find him watching TV on the couch holding his ferret, who pooped everywhere (the ferret, not Marcus). The house always smelled of urine and ferret poop, but even when we cleaned, we couldn't get rid of the smell. Finally, when Mom got rid of Marcus, we moved her bed for some reason and found that the ferret had made its way behind the drawers that were under it. Lo and behold, we now understood why the house still smelled, due to the piles and piles of feces. We had to throw out the entire bed frame because we couldn't get the stench out.

Participant number two was Robert. He had a crew cut and a dark beard, muscular from working construction most of his life, and very combative. He didn't talk much and had a face that seemed to be weighed down by something heavier than life itself; if we played too loud, he'd yell and grab you by the arm to get your attention.

The breakfast menu for me and Pat would have a small list of church food box items to choose from; cereal (puffed wheat or rice), sugar or honey, and the 50/50 mix of powdered and whole milk. If you've never had puffed wheat or rice, it's like eating Styrofoam balls out of a beanbag chair. We'd add lots of sugar or honey to make it palatable. I didn't often complain about what we had to eat, although working my way through the plate could take hours if onions, broccoli, or brussels sprouts were on the menu. Pat, however, wanted everyone to know he wasn't happy.

One fateful day, as always, we poured bowls of puffed wheat with more than a spoonful of sugar and began to eat.

After a few bites, Pat said, "I can't. I really can't eat this again. It's so disgusting!"

Robert was in the kitchen with us packing his lunch and he heard what Pat said. Without saying a word, he marched over and shoved Pat's face into the bowl. "You'll eat what you're given, you ungrateful brat!" Robert yelled as he held Pat's face down.

It seemed like minutes passed as I watched Pat's arms flail around, in his attempt to catch his breath and get away from Robert. Finally, the man let go of my big brother's head. Pat's face was bright red with anger and embarrassment, and he sat there with milk and tears dripping down his face, as we finished our meal in silence.

When Mom came home and Robert explained what had happened, she told us, "It serves you right. You don't talk back to adults."

We already knew that though; listen, and be good. Mom had lightning reflexes if one of us said something sassy, so you always wanted to be more than an arm's length away from her, with plenty of room to move. She could reach into the back seat of the car and spank you with one hand while steering with the other. There was no warning, just a loud thud announcing the beginning of a bloody nose or mouth. You didn't overreact, you took the punishment she handed out. Mom acted like it was her right to discipline us this way. If you had a bruise, a fat lip, or anything else that showed the battle scar of her wrath, she would say, "If you didn't move, it wouldn't be so bad."

When Pat and I got up the next morning, Robert was gone. Mom's excuse was that he had to help his daughter with something in another state. She didn't talk to Pat about what happened to him, instead she just told us that Robert had to go. Either way, there were plenty of other men at the Post Time Pub who would find their way into our home soon enough.

As we lived in Tucson, there was always an open desert nearby to get away from the house, and we'd run into friends from school or church who were doing the same thing we were. One day, we had been walking in the desert for a few minutes when we heard someone call out our names. It was a teenage boy from church who always gave me a strange feeling in my stomach when I saw him. He was one of the oldest kids in the Royal Rangers, but this time, he looked different. As he said hello and smiled, a strange feeling in my stomach led my eyes to his chest and muscular arms exposed by his tank top. I tried to stop looking, but there was something that fascinated about him. It was the same feeling I'd had with some of the boys in my class over the past few years.

He was with a group of his high school friends and suggested we join them. They were doing more mature things than playing in the desert. One of the other guys had arrived with a picnic basket, which seemed a little silly.

Then another guy said, "Did you bring it?" and he opened the basket to reveal a stack of porn magazines.

They pulled a few out and began to flip through them. I had seen magazines like these before, always accompanied by that weird feeling.

Pat paused for a moment to look, then looked at me and made the excuse that we were meeting some other friends and had to leave. Everyone was too engrossed in what they were looking at and said a half-uttered "bye." Then we went to find other kids to play with.

Pat made friends a lot easier than I did, and as we got older, our friend groups looked different. He was more adventurous and athletic than I was, so his group of friends reflected that. Sometimes these adventures were not exactly legal and a little on the nose for him. One long weekend, right after school was out, he and his friend were caught jumping on the roof of the junior high school across the street from our apartment and playing in the courtyards when school wasn't in session. The janitor who caught them called the cops; another breach in the Carnie Code. That was the last straw for Mom. She called Tom to tell him what was happening and demanded that he find a way for us to stay with him for the coming summer.

I couldn't understand why she would send us to live with a man she had spoken so horribly about. Although being around Mom caused extreme amounts of anxiety and stress, it was my normal. Leaving our home in Tucson and the small group of friends I had added to the stress, and I was overwhelmed by the idea of going to stay with Tom. I urged Mom not to make me go, and she finally relented and let Pat go alone. I would stay home all by myself since Pennie was now in Phoenix and Sis had her own group of high school friends.

My summer was a bit of a blur, with Mom working and Sis going back and forth from her boyfriend's house. I got to see a few friends, swam at the apartment pool, went to church, and received a list of chores to complete each day. It was lonely not having Pat around, and I couldn't wait for my brother to come home from the carnival.

The sixth grade took us to a new part of town, which meant another new school. This was the first time Pat and I would be separated, as he was off to Junior High. I started at a Spanish immersion school, where the first half of the day was in Spanish and the second half was in English. At this time, Tucson was facing an increase in its non-English speaking Hispanic population, so they were trying to solve the education problem quickly and identified my school for a pilot. It was a progressive idea that was challenged from both sides of the political landscape, putting kids center stage to determine what were the right and wrong ways of approaching educating Spanish speakers. Two-thirds of the class was Spanish-speaking only, and they looked as scared as I did. Mom made the situation worse since she had a lot of negative assumptions about anyone who wasn't white. 'They' were the cause of all the bad things that were happening in society. I'd had several Black and Latino friends at my previous school, but because of what my mom said about them, there was still a belief that maybe there was something wrong with them.

When the year started, my world changed quickly. The teacher immediately started speaking in Spanish and gave a few cues to the small group of non-Spanish speakers on what we were doing. I had no idea what was going on and by the end of the first week, I didn't want to go back. I didn't hear any of the other students say they were struggling, so I felt dumb that I wasn't picking up the Spanish part of class. Once again, I felt unheard and left out. By the end of week two, my frustration about not learning fast enough turned to anger at the kids that were 'making me do it.' Since I knew how Mom felt about other races, I complained about not being accepted by the other kids. I lied that they were mean to me, I had no friends, and the teacher wasn't helping me. In true Mom fashion, she responded to the false injustice I had conjured up by explosively ranting to the principal that her child was not getting the education he deserved and that she would be pulling me out of the school. Mom was able to enroll me in my original school near Nana's house. This created a new problem since there wasn't another school within walking distance, so the Sun Tran public bus system would become my new transportation. Even to this day, I hold deep regret for how I lied about the students, teachers, and school. I saw them as mom did. I capitalized on her dislike for people not like her to get my way. Everyone at that school was actually kind and trying their best with the situation. Adulthood has allowed me to change my perspective and own my wrongs.

Along with a new school and places to explore, Mom introduced boyfriend number three, a suicidal alcoholic named Richard. We went through the normal awkward introductions we had been through so many times before. She would sit us down, tell us that she had met someone who was going to move in, and then later that day she would bring him home. Richard was another guy who didn't have a job, but he collected cans from the garbage to get enough money for the next bottle to drink.

Richard seemed to contribute to the family pretty quickly, though. We would go to bed with barely any food in the fridge, but in the morning, it would be mostly full of yogurt, soda, and canned vegetables in the cupboards. We were thrilled because Mom never bought name brands. A few weeks later, Mom was working double shifts, and Richard asked Pat and me if we would like to go collecting cans with him. He said he would reward us by buying us Dairy Queen afterward, so, of course, we jumped right in. The first stop was the dumpsters in our apartment complex, where we tore open bags to find empty cans. The smell of rotting food, diapers, and whatever else steeped in the summer heat buried itself in the depths of our nostrils and the back of our throats.

Our next stop was the grocery store around the corner from our apartment. We pulled up and jumped into the commercial-sized dumpster the store used to dispose of expired meats, fruits, vegetables, canned goods, and dairy products.

As Pat and I started looking for aluminum cans, Richard said, "Don't go past those containers, that food is still good. The store just had to throw it out."

We gathered the yogurt containers, canned food, and soda and set them on the ledge of the dumpster, so Richard could put them in a box he had in the back of the car. We finished looking for aluminum cans and then moved on to the next dumpster. Once we had three bags of cans, we headed to the recycling center, strategically located across the street from the Dairy Queen. Butterfinger and Oreo Blizzards were all Pat and I could think about. Richard gave us ten dollars and we ran across the street to enjoy the fruits of our labor. Once our cups were totally empty, we got back in the car and headed home to refill our fridge and cupboards with the reclaimed waste we had found in the dumpster.

After a few months of Richard living with us, he married Mom. We learned of the happy occasion when Richard woke us in the middle of the night as he tried to hug us and said incoherently, "I love you. I'm going to be your dad." I pushed him away. The next morning, Mom was up early and confirmed the events of the night before.

We'd spend a few weeks in the awkward state of Richard trying to play a father role while drunk. Pat and I kept our distance, mostly because he smelled like old vomit. He'd have bouts of depression and pass out on the couch for a few days. It had become so overwhelming for him that he had attempted suicide by using a broken bottle to cut three bloody lines on each arm, from wrist to elbow. Mom knew what would happen if she took him to the hospital, so she bandaged his wounds with maxi pads and gauze, then stayed home to watch him until he sobered up. Richard stayed sober for about two weeks. I think it was mostly because he couldn't go out looking for cans to cash in. Besides, no one would sell liquor to a man bandaged from wrist to elbow. Within a couple of weeks, Mom either got tired of him or couldn't find him when she went out at night. He just kind of disappeared. And my mom didn't even say anything; we just didn't see him anymore.

After Richard disappeared, we moved through a couple of trailer parks where Mom would find a single random guy that would frequent our house. At first, we lived in a small travel trailer with a long seat in the front where Pat and I sat on opposite ends to sleep. Mom and Sis shared the bed in the back. We got reacquainted with the Sun Tran bus schedule so we could get to school and not fall behind time or school activities. Mom eventually 'made friends' with the park's landlord who helped her get a bigger trailer across the aisle, where Pat and I could have our own beds. We lived there for several months, but when Mom broke up with the guy, we quickly had to pack up and move to another apartment.

Summer was fast approaching, which meant it was time to go to the carnival with Tom. I began to formulate my plans to stay home. For weeks, I begged Mom, promising to be good, to take care of myself, and stay out of the way – but to no avail. One early morning, we arrived in Williams, AZ. The midway was still quiet as everyone slept in their beds. Mom navigated the trailers set up behind the carnival to find Tom's. When she found it, she returned with a groggy, bed-headed man ready to help carry our garbage-bag luggage to his summer abode, where Pat and I would share a bed.

I was old enough to contribute so I played a role in the carnival economy. I was asked to run a new lemonade stand next to the food wagons. It was in a screened-in, bright yellow wooden square with "Fresh Lemonade" painted on three sides. I had two ten-gallon igloo coolers, a water hose, lemon juice, and sugar to make it. It should have been easy to follow the instructions on the back of the bottle, but I could never get it right. One container would be too sweet and the other too sour. It was okay when I was working alone because I could figure out the balance between the two. But during the hot summers, there would be long lines of people during the day, so the big boss's daughter would jump in to help.

We had been on the road for several weeks and had begun to learn the ins and outs of carnival life. You got one or two showers a week, and if your clothes didn't have a stain on them, then they are clean. There was usually drinking after the show closed for the evening, which gave Pat and me easy access to try whatever we wanted – mostly flavored liquor or beer, neither of which tasted very good. Dinner was usually at a Denny's or JB's restaurant since Tom's trailer was such a mess that we couldn't get to the two-burner stove. Breakfast would be one of those little boxes of cereal they serve at restaurants or a packaged pastry from the convenience store. Powdered doughnuts and chocolate milk were my go-to. We had no idea what a vegetable or fruit looked like the entire time we were on the road. Although we were clearly still children, we were expected to act like grown men, show up on time, ready to work, and take direction without talking back. Tom gave us total freedom and treated us as equals instead of like his kids. But though it was fun to have the freedom to do literally anything I wanted, I missed the comfort and structure of home.

When Sis and her boyfriend, David, came to visit us in Prescott, I told her what we had been up to for the past few weeks. Then I told her that I really missed home and begged them to take me with them. This was certainly not the plan for either of them; it was supposed to be a day trip to get out of the heat. Yet, after a few hours of talking to Mom, convincing David, and telling Tom, they agreed to take me.

Back home in Tucson, I made myself comfortable on the living room couch of Sis and David's apartment for the rest of the summer. When school was about to start, Mom found another one bedroom apartment and collected her two boys. Then contestant number four, Roger, was ready to be introduced to us, already waiting at home. Roger was a former martial arts champion and military man. Built like a kung fu master, he was super lean and had quick reflexes, which he used to horse around with us. Even the slightest touch from him would cause a level of pain like he was pulling your soul out through your eye socket. If he got too rough with us, we could hit him as hard as we could and he'd just sit there like nothing happened. He could really take a beating.

Roger loved popcorn and feeding the ducks at Reid Park. Almost every day, we'd come home from school to a pot of popcorn, half for the ducks and half for us. We'd make regular trips to the lakes with him to feed the ducks. Roger really seemed to care about us. Mom worked so much that he was a bit of a caretaker as well. He was the one there in the morning when we went to school, and he made dinner for us in the evening. He didn't work because he was on military disability. He was a smart guy and could talk about what was going on in the news and sports – which I didn't really care about – or just talk about the day. It felt normal to have him there waiting for us when school was over.

Puberty arrived in our house like a train barreling down open tracks. With Pat and I only a year apart, hormones and hard-ons were a constant. We had no idea what it all meant, even after the standard sex-ed class from fifth grade. Roger would have the wonderful task of talking to us about sex and our changing bodies.

One night, the three of us had just finished dinner when Roger cleared his throat and said, "So...your bodies are changing."

We had a wide-eyed conversation about body hair, deodorant, our balls dropping, deeper voices, masturbation, and girls. Although we had seen sex in dirty magazines, no one had ever addressed it out loud. Now, this man we barely knew was talking about it all so openly. It was strange and comforting.

Roger was a kind man, and whether he wanted to or not, he filled in some fatherly gaps for me. He said he was proud of me and patted us on the back when we needed encouragement. He was the one who comforted me when my dog died and dug a hole in the backyard, in the rain to bury her. He was actually a positive male role model, not like the previous men Mom had brought home. I wanted Roger to be a permanent part of our home. He was becoming the buffer between Mom, me and Pat, which was a relief. Although I never sat next to him on the couch to snuggle in to watch TV, I was way too old for that, I wanted to be around him. I felt like he was actually parenting us, but he was choosing to be presenting. The anxiety I regularly felt with just Mom around began to settle. There was some emotional space to solely be a kid, play video games, ride bikes, and get Thrifty ice cream. Roger cared about me. It didn't feel like he was trying to replace Tom, he was just sharing what he had learned and wished someone had shared with him.

He lived with us for about a year, and everything seemed to be going well. Then suddenly, things went south. Pat and I had gone to school, said goodbye to Roger, and when we came back, he was gone, just like the expanding list of others that had been erased from our home: Tom, Pennie, and countless men. We got no explanation as to where or why he had gone. Mom just said he wasn't coming back, as she went into the kitchen to start making dinner.

Before we knew it, school was out and we were making arrangements to join Tom in Northern Arizona. The summer of my seventh-grade year brought me to the big time; running a joint – which is what we called a game at the carnival. My joint wasn't very complicated. All you had to do was shoot the ball into a basket about chest high and four to five feet away. It wasn't for the superstar basketball player, but for kids and non-athletes, kind of like me. There's a belief that all carnival games are rigged, but for the life of me, I couldn't figure out how this one would have been. The hoop and backboards were standard. It wasn't misshapen or tilted, but people always had a hard time making the basket.

Different characters came to the show in each city. They all had a story about what brought them there. We had just arrived in Gallup, New Mexico, when a tall, thin woman with a flowing scarf covering her bald head showed up looking for a job. The joint boss talked to her about her experience, where she was from, and explained the Carnie Code. She had a great personality – always smiling and flirting with the men who passed by to get them to come over and play her game – so she quickly fit in with 'the family.'

That summer was sweltering. We had set up in a grocery store parking lot, so the heat just radiated off the pavement. With no AC in the trailer, Pat and I decided to move from our shared bed inside to a makeshift bed outside. We set up in the back of Tom's truck to at least get a little breeze when it blew by. It was normal to hear voices in passing while you slept, even the occasional drunken brawl, so we rarely thought much about it. Being in the back of the truck, however, made us aware of many more sounds.

Suddenly, we heard a woman scream, "No, I'm not going. You can't take me."

Then another group of people responded. At first, it seemed to be the normal carnie disagreement, but it kept escalating. Pat and I tried to figure out who it was so we could tell them to shut up and go to sleep. When we sat up, we saw it was the bald scarf lady standing by her car with the door open, pointing a revolver at the cops.

We were thirty feet away, in full view of her yelling, "I'm not going!" as she shot at them. Then she jumped in the car and slammed on the accelerator, heading straight for them. At the last minute, she swerved and crashed into a drainage ditch where the car stopped, and the cops pulled her out and threw her on the ground. She was struggling and cursing them the whole time. We could still hear her screaming after they put her in the back of the cop car.

The next day, the big boss brought everyone together. He explained that the bald scarf-lady had shot her boyfriend and was on the run. He reminded us all of two things; one, no cops; and two, respect the code. He said, "Don't bring the cops; if you have problems with them, you better leave now because I don't want them on my midway." We all acknowledged the Carnie Code and went about our business of preparing for the opening.

When summer was finally over, Mom met us in Flagstaff for the kid exchange. Pat and I, with our clothes in large black trash bags, summer finds, and money in our pockets, headed down the mountains with her, back to the desert of Tucson to get ready for the start of the next school year. Some of the money we earned would go directly to Mom for school supplies and clothes. The big reward for me was using the last one hundred and twenty-five dollars I had to buy an original Nintendo, Super Mario Bros, and Duck Hunt. Playing those games on our thirteen-inch black and white TV was worth every minute I spent on the road that summer.

As we rounded the last curve on Interstate 10 through the outskirts of Tucson, Mom mentioned that she hadn't found a place for us to live yet. Luckily, Sis and David had agreed to let us stay with them until she got settled.

Sis or Darlene Kay is the second oldest kid and six years older than me. She was always the free-spirited one and a little accident-prone. She wore makeup as soon as she was allowed and listened to great music like Bon Jovi, Air Supply, and Madonna. She was a performer in school plays and choir, dated the cute guy in high school, was a little aloof about life, and loved the color purple. She was the lefty of the family until I came along. She was so passionate about it that she forced me to use my right hand. It worked, and may be why I have such horrible handwriting; thanks Sis! She can hustle like Mom and will make sure her kids are always taken care of. She is independent and crafty as a way of finding her center.

At Sis', we all lived in a one-bedroom apartment, where Pat and I once again cozied up on opposite ends of the living room couch. David was a nice guy – handsome, fit, funny, adventurous, and a hard worker. He regularly walked around without a shirt on, which clearly showed the manual labor he put in, and I got that weird feeling in my stomach again. It reminded me of that feeling when I saw the guy in the tank top. I'd only heard guys talk about that feeling when they saw a pretty girl and instinctively knew it wasn't something I could talk about, so I just ignored it. We had a lot of freedom to keep ourselves busy while Sis and David were away. We wasted our time swimming in the apartment pool, watching David's porn collection and stealing dimes from an oversized beer can he kept in their bedroom.

I was enrolled in eighth grade at Amphi Junior High, where I began to discover my passions at school. I took woodworking, learned to use power tools, and in home economics I learned to cook and sew. I picked up sewing pretty easily, maybe because I regularly saw Mom at her sewing machine, mending clothes or making something.

Pat and I rode the public bus to school since we lived outside the district. Most of the time, I was on my own on the way home since he had a different school schedule. However, there was always a guy from Pat's school on my bus. He told me that his dad had taught him how to shave, and now he had to do it once a month. He was hoping to grow a beard when he got older. He leaned over and said, "You got a lot of peach fuzz, you got to shave that off, man." I left the bus embarrassed that I hadn't even noticed and immediately went home to stare in the mirror, wondering how to get rid of it. I had seen a couple of TV shows where the dad shaved, but that didn't really help. That night, I worked up the courage to ask David how to shave. He was always a bit of a jerk, overly cocky, and still resting on his popularity from high school which was now appearing further and further away.

He leaned in to look at my face, laughed at me, and said, "Do you have hairy balls now?" He wrestled me to the ground and pulled up my shirt to pull at my armpit hair, then pushed me away. He finally gave in and said, "Yeah, I'll show you this weekend."

The experience was pretty basic; razor, shaving cream, which way to pull the blade, etc. When I was done, he walked away, I washed my face, and I stood there, my face feeling so smooth and a little sore. I stared into the mirror while the thought of being a man lingered in my mind. *Is this it?* I thought. Everything that defined a man was boiled down to a shaving lesson and the previous awkward conversation with Roger. Funny how something so small can make such a big difference in a young person's mind.

Mom found another trailer for us to live in. Pat and I shared one room while Mom and her boyfriend shared the other. That moved us to another school and back into the cycle of making new friends. Pat had a mattress to sleep on where he could settle in with his old red, white-and-black plaid blanket. I slept on an oversized stuffed mat that lay directly on the floor. I hadn't seen my best friend, Matt, in several months so we had worked out for him to come over and stay the night. We walked around the trailer park and I pointed out where some of my friends lived. When we returned home, we wanted to play video games, so we went back to my room.

When he walked into the sparsely furnished space, he noticed our beds and then asked why mine was on the floor and so thin. That was the first time I realized that my home life was very different from my friends', especially Matt's. Most homes had a mom and dad, with a car that worked, and food in the fridge. Most kids didn't need someone to sponsor them to go to church camp or an event. Now seeing through a wider lens of life, things changed for me that day, not because Matt said something about my bed, but because I became fully aware of how poor we really were.

As the school year ended, I knew that living with Tom for the summer would be twice as difficult as living at home in Tucson. I was so much more aware of the small, dirty trailer, the constant travel, the drugs, alcohol, and fights that were part of the carnie life. I didn't want to go, even if it meant spending the whole summer alone. I would rather be alone than live like that, but I didn't think I could convince Mom to change her mind, so I braced for what was to come.

Earlier in the year, Sis and David decided to move to Florida to spend more time with his mom. They'd packed up his red Ford Ranger and headed for their new life. Sis had only been in Florida a few months when she mysteriously returned with her son, Erik, and stayed in Tucson with friends. No sooner than getting settled, Sis had decided to go back to Florida to be with David again. It was perfect timing for Mom to send me off with her to babysit Erik while Sis worked. So, it was decided for me; I wouldn't be staying in Tucson, but trekking across the U.S. with Sis and Erik to join David.

We packed our bags, boarded a Greyhound bus, and spent two and a half days driving a straight line across the southern half of the United States from Tucson to Tampa. If you've never traveled across the U.S. by bus, it's an unforgettable experience. It's kind of like cramming all carnie characters into one vehicle, without food or a functional bathroom. You meet all kinds of people who live life loudly, even in close proximity. We saw fights over seats, people smoking pot, and 'getting to know' each other. We only paid for two seats because Erik was about six months old, but he still needed to move around and sleep. The second night on the bus he was cranky and needed to stretch out. The bus was completely full, so I laid him across the seat and sat on the floor with my hand on his back to make sure he didn't roll off. Time couldn't go fast enough for us to get off the bus. It was smelly, sticky, and I'm sure carried enough bacteria to give you a disease. When we arrived in Tampa, David picked us up at a bus stop next to a pawnshop and strip club on the outskirts of town. We all piled into his single bench seat truck and drove to Bradenton. This would be my new home, one of many I'd had in my short life. David had a roommate, so Sis, David, and Erik slept in the master bedroom, the other guy in the second bedroom, and I had my regular landing spot; another couch.

Sis quickly found a job, which meant I started my new work as a babysitter. Everyday David and Sis would go to work and I would take care of Erik. Having lived in Tucson most of my life, I thought Florida would be a tropical retreat, but all it offered was relentless rain every afternoon and a constant sweat from head to toe. It was like clockwork; every afternoon the heavens would turn on the faucet and it would rain for about forty-five minutes. Erik and I would just sit and watch the rain as part of our daily entertainment.

You couldn't stay on the floor in the house for very long because David's dog had brought fleas home. This made it even miserable to sleep after the roommate left when I moved into the second bedroom. I didn't have a bed, so I slept on a sheet on the floor with those flees disturbing my rest. Every night was a constant agony of tiny bites. When I woke up in the morning, it was like the end of a big locust invasion, with them jumping all over me. Bradenton, Florida, wasn't too bad, though; it felt like an adventure every time we went out. The beaches were warm with pockets of trees and grass. The harbor had so many jellyfish it seemed like there was more jelly than water, and the snakes, ugh, there were so many they had their own crosswalk. To a thirteen-year-old boy, it was all a wonderland.

Now being a teenager, I was becoming more aware of my surroundings and understanding of the dynamics in a room. After a month in Florida, David started drinking a lot and the yelling started. It became a regular occurrence. It felt like I was back home with Mom. The berating, the feeling of not being welcome, and the occasional smack on the backside of my head.

One afternoon, I was in the front living room with Erik and an argument started in the bedroom. I heard Sis say, "Stop, let me go." There was more back and forth yelling and he started calling her names. Sis told him to stop hurting her. I could hear her crying and repeating, "You're hurting me... stop...David, stop."

I put Erik down and went back into the room. As I walked in, David was holding Sis with one arm and hitting her with a high-heeled shoe with the other.

I yelled, "Stop! Stop hitting my sister." He jumped off the bed, told me to shut up and backhanded me square in the left temple with his class ring. The blow was so hard that it knocked me against the wall, and I fell to the floor. My head was immediately in excruciating pain. I crawled into my room to hide, which seemed to stop their fight. I lay there crying for hours, finding nothing or no one to comfort my pain. I could hear them mumbling through the wall, but my head hurt so much that it was hard to concentrate on what they were saying. The soft tones of their voices became rhythmic until I fell asleep on the floor. When I woke up, my left template was swollen, accompanied by a large bruise that covered half of my eye, and I felt nauseous. I vomited over and over for the next few hours. In between quick naps, I laid on the sheet that covered the carpet to form the outline of a bed.

I could hear David in the bathroom complaining about me being sick, "What the hell is wrong with him?"

Sis replied, "You fucking hit him in the head, David. He probably has a concussion."

The next few days were difficult because my head was throbbing whenever I was upright. When I finally emerged three days after the incident, Sis looked at me with tears in her eyes and said, "We're going home." That was it; we started packing up David's Hot Wheel-sized Ford Ranger truck. Then all four of us got in the truck to go home. Except for communicating the need for an occasional pee or food break, we drove twenty-two hours to Phoenix in utter silence.

Since I was with Sis in Florida, Mom assumed I wasn't coming back to Tucson, so there was nothing to keep her there. Earlier in the summer, she had reconnected with some old carnie friends who had moved to California. She'd mentioned that she was looking for work and they offered her a job at the county fair. When we abruptly returned to Arizona, there was no way to reach her to make plans for me when we arrived. Instead, Sis arranged for us to stay with Nonnie and her family. As David pulled his truck into her driveway, we quickly set about unpacking what little we had. He didn't say anything as we brought in the last of the boxes. There was no apology, no remorse. It was as if he was a taxi driver, dropping us off at our destination. Instead, he just turned and left. Sis shared a room with Nonnie's youngest daughter. Another couch had my name on it for whatever timeline this story would hold.

At this point, the swelling on my head had begun to subside. The bruise was slightly green around the edges, indicating signs of healing, but that was the furthest thing from true for my heart. Within a week, Sis told me she was going back to Tucson to be with David, and I was to stay with Nonnie. I was shocked. Why would she go back to live with him after what had happened? There was no way this had been the first time. How could she be okay with him hitting her like that? Would he do that to Erik? Could he do worse? Sis' departure was another blow to the temple, where a sensitive knot had begun to form. I was thirteen years old, had no one I could count on, and was left with a cliffhanger for what would happen to Joey next. It's a good story now, but hell, it's a shitty story for a kid.

Nonnie comforted me when Sis left. I had no connection with Pennie for the whole summer, and Pat had gone off with his dad, probably having the time of his life. Maybe I should have gone with him, I thought. Within a few days, Mom sent for me. Nonnie and I went to the local travel agency and bought a ticket to San Jose, CA. It was my first time on an airplane. The agent was excited to explain the adventure I was about to embark on. Little did she know that my entire life already had so many twists and turns that a two-and-a-half-hour flight wouldn't have a significant impact on me. She handed Nonnie the ticket and slipped a piece of gum into the envelope to remind me to chew it as the plane took off.

Final Thoughts

Throughout my childhood, I lived in a constant state of survival. Not knowing what the next day would bring made it difficult for me to feel safe, and it wore on my mind and spirit. Settling into my seat on the plane, I unwrapped the piece of gum the agent had given me and then closed my eyes to settle in for the flight. As I rested my eyes, I was drawn back to playing in the Tucson desert. Those lighter moments of being a kid, racing from bush to bush in a game of hide-and-seek, chasing roadrunners and rabbits, feeling carefree. But that wasn't life anymore. Staying quiet about the abuse I had witnessed a few weeks before, the prospect of another round at carnival life, and being on my way back to Mom forced me to retreat even more. Like the midsummer desert of my childhood, my soul was withered and parched from lack of nourishment for my heart. I'd tried so hard to be good, but still could not find the acceptance and belonging I craved. Even with the glimpse of refreshing encouragement from Royal Ranger leaders, friends, church and school teachers, and even Roger, there wasn't much of Joey left to revive.

Part Two

Cali

When I landed in San Jose, I looked for the signature blonde beehive we were so accustomed to. Mom was waiting for me at the gate to sweep me off to her next county fair. Once we got there, she checked in with her boss who told her she could drive over to the fairgrounds and start setting up her booth. But before I could join, I had to enroll in a local school to get a work permit. We went to the closest one and filled out the paperwork to start school the next month, though there were no plans for me to actually start at that school. In addition to the 'new school' she enrolled me in, Mom also gave me a new name: "You're too old to be called Joey. You're going to be Joe now." Having learned the hard way that there was no talking back or arguing with her, I acknowledged her statement and moved on.

Mom had been working for a custom hat vendor, and now I would be working with her. After people finished visiting the animals and watching the rodeo, they wanted to be just like the crowned queen. Most men would look for a standard felt cowboy hat, which we could steam on site to fit. Most of the customers bought cowboy hats, but there were a few Crocodile Dundy styles that we kept in the corner. The star of the show was a rodeo queen's cowboy hat. The hat itself was white, which we spray-painted with light blues, pinks, purples, and finished with a feather trim hot-glued around the brim. Customers would come to our booth and get measured for their own hat. If we didn't have the color they wanted, it only took a few minutes to paint a new one and I'd run out to customize it. We could charge a few extra dollars for customization, so it was worth the extra few minutes.

One day, two men approached us to buy hats for themselves and their girlfriends, who were elsewhere at the fair. They gave us an American Express credit card to pay the one-hundred-dollar bill. Before we processed the card with the aluminum machine that imprints the number on the carbon paper, I ran to a nearby payphone to get authorization for the card. When I returned, Mom was packing up the hats and the men were waving goodbye.

Late the next day, Mom's boss showed up and asked her to step outside to talk for a minute. I continued to set up for the day, occasionally looking up to see when she was returning. As Mom came around the corner, her eyes were fixed on the booth. She walked in double time with determination in her short legs; I could see that she was upset. She picked up her things and said, "Let's go, son." Mom had been fired because the credit card we accepted the day before was stolen. In the grand scheme of things, the loss of a hundred dollars probably wasn't that big of a deal to this boss man, but it was the principle of a loss, so he fired us.

Always knowing how to hustle and make connections, Mom had a list of people in the address book she kept in her purse that she could call to see where her next gig might start. She connected with a friend who knew of a county fair that was about to open in Paso Robles and gave her a contact she could talk to. So Mom gassed up her 1973 Chevy Impala and we drove south through the night, arriving fairly early the next day. Tearing down everything on Sunday night and sometimes driving straight to the next destination in the middle of the night to get there on Monday afternoon was part of carnie life. Mom was certainly used to driving and even working through the night, so she caffeinated up, took a couple of NoDoze, and we set our sights down to central California.

When we arrived in Paso Robles, Mom went straight to meet another 'Big Boss' who knew she was coming. She told me to walk around for a few minutes while they talked. I strolled up and down the midway, watching the jocks assemble their rides with small cranes to lift metal seats into place and lock them in place with a mouse key. It was only a few minutes before I saw Mom coming down the same aisle, with a slight smirk on her face, her little legs carrying her body quickly toward me with her head held high. This time, I could see a sense of pride in her spirit. I could tell that she had landed her next gig.

We jumped back in the car and drove to the next town, Atascadero, where her friend, Carol, lived. After a few hours of catching up and me getting acquainted with her, Carol offered us a place to stay while Mom worked her next gig. Once again, I settled down on someone's couch.

When Mom headed off to work, I was left to explore the one-acre lot where Carol lived with her dogs, then made my way up and down the street. Carol's house was halfway up a hill, so no matter which way you walked, you'd have to climb back up to get home. I figured that out pretty quickly. Carol's husband was a distant truck driver and was rarely home, so Mom shared a room with Carol. Her mother-in-law, whom we called Ma, was from Maine and spoke with a thick Northeastern accent, although she had been in California for at least twenty years. Finally, a gay couple, Chris and Mike, came and went through another entrance to the house. They rented the room right next to the dining room, and the only thing separating the two was a plastic accordion-style door.

As the fair ended, I prepared to pack up again, but Mom had made an alternate plan. She explained that she had to keep working, and Carol had agreed to let me stay there to start my freshman year. I was used to Mom leaving, so it wasn't much of a surprise. However, I didn't like the idea of her leaving me with strangers. There was no way to change her mind, so in my obedient style, I said "okay." The next day, Mom packed her things, hugged me goodbye, and reminded me to "listen and be good," and left.

As the start of the school year approached, Carol took me to the local KMart to buy supplies and clothes, then to Payless Shoes to find look-alike Nike high-tops. It was another year of a new school and a totally different style of kids. I rode my bike four miles through the hills of Atascadero and finally arrived at the hill where the school sat. Then I walked into campus to begin the process of making new friends, learning where my classes were and the social norms for the student body. I decided to work in the library for one of my elective hours. The three librarians were like my newfound grandmas and made the transition to this new place bearable. What's more, I was grafted into a group of friends who were fun to hang out with.

Life at home was pretty quiet. Carol and Ma worked regular jobs, so I was home alone for several hours in the afternoon. It was usually nice to do homework and explore the hills. Carol allowed me to use a motorized scooter to venture farther from home and really experience the winding roads, up and down the hills on back roads, and past countless Christmas tree farms. Having this level of freedom was new to me, life had been so heavy up to that point. She didn't have many rules, but her only rule was to be kind and respectful. The weight of worrying about upsetting someone or not following the rules began to lift, which helped me start to enjoy school and home-life.

The couple who lived in the next room always said "hello" every morning and evening. As far as I knew, I had never been around a gay person before, so I was fascinated and curious. It seemed natural for them to hold hands, kiss, and sit closely together. Mike engaged more with us in the day-to-day, and he would occasionally join us for dinner while Chris was at work. As I looked across the dinner table on one of those nights, I got the same strange feeling in my stomach that I had when I'd seen the guy in the tank top a few years before. Mike was a well-dressed guy with wavy hair and a nice smile. Could it be that he was attractive? Was it okay to actually feel this way, or was there something wrong with me? These weren't new feelings, I was just becoming more aware of them as I entered my teenage years. I didn't really know what to do with them, though. Mom was very clear about who 'those' people were, and that we shouldn't hang out with them. Now, I lived in the same house with them and they didn't seem as bad as Mom had made it sound. Yet, I was still afraid to talk about what was going on inside my head, especially now that it was coming up more regularly – especially in weightlifting class and when watching the water polo team practice. I had to follow the rules and "be good," though, so I pushed those feelings and thoughts farther away, so I didn't have to deal with them.

Mom was now living with Aunt Darlene and she invited me to Phoenix to celebrate Christmas with them. Carol dropped me off at the Greyhound bus stop before dawn, and gave me a hug, some snacks, and a few dollars to buy something extra if I wanted. Twelve hours later, I arrived at the Phoenix bus station where Mom was waiting for me. Her blonde beehive hair singled her out before she had a chance to wave me down. She gave me a quick hug and asked me how the trip went. Then we walked to the car and headed for her new home.

Aunt Darlene had always held a special place in my heart, going back to when she came to Tucson for Christmas and stopped by to say hello to our family. The thought of seeing her again made me feel both excited and comforted.

When we walked into the trailer, she was there with a warm hug and the obligatory "you're so tall" and "I feel really old." She peppered me with questions that slowly broke down the walls I had so carefully built. I could talk to her about almost anything. Pat had been staying with a friend from the carnival who needed to put down roots so her own kids could start school. Mom picked him up so we could all be together. We spent three fantastic days at Aunt Darlene's; went to church, celebrated Christmas, and saw my sisters who were also in Phoenix.

In just three days, I had reconnected with someone who truly cared about me, who I was, and who I hoped to become. But as quickly as I had arrived, it was already time to leave. As if the vacation had been put on rewind, I packed my bags, said my goodbyes, and Mom took me back to the bus station. Before Mom could see me start to cry, I hugged her. As always, she said, "Listen and be good." Then, I boarded the bus and began the slow trek back to Atascadero. I arrived late that night but Carol and Ma were there waiting for me. Their welcome was warm, with a hint of relief that I was back. Although I would have liked to stay with Aunt Darlene or even go with Pat, it felt nice to be missed, comforted, and welcomed home.

Soon, I transitioned back to school and home life with Carol and Ma. Occasionally, Carol's husband would come home from weeks on the road, and we'd celebrate his arrival with dinner. When he left again, the three of us would enjoy road trips to Morrow Rock on the coast, San Luis Obispo for the farmers market, and Santa Barbara for a Costco run. Although I felt comfortable at Carol's house, I continued to think about my time with Aunt Darlene and longed to be back in Phoenix where I could see her. After a few months, I came home from school one day to find Carol waiting for me. She said my mom had called and would be coming to pick me up. My wish had come true: I was going to live with her at Aunt Darlene's. Carol seemed upset and Ma stayed in her room much longer than usual for the next few days. There was sadness in the air as I packed my things. Carol and Ma had given so much to me. The anxiety I had felt around Mom had disappeared. Even in the awkwardness of my teenage body, I had a group of friends, a stable home life, and people who showed me love. Now, that was being erased, another new home, although one that I wanted to experience, I would have to rebuild the walls that had taken months to come down if I was going to be around Mom again.

The enormous brown Impala pulling into the driveway announced Mom's arrival. She was accompanied by a man in the passenger seat and Pat's head was sticking out of the back seat. When the car came to a stop, they all alighted and stretched as if they had been crammed into a clown car for hours, took deep breaths, and came inside. The energy between Mom and Carol made it clear that something wasn't right, but they exchanged the usual pleasantries as we made our way inside. Mom proudly introduced her new boyfriend, a cross-eyed, severely overweight man who spoke with a lisp. I didn't really care who he was, I knew she'd soon move on from this guy anyway.

Introducing Pat to the large German Shepherd that lived with us gave me a chance to ask, "So, who's the weirdo with Mom?"

"Ah, just another dork that Mom met on a whim," he sighed.

It wasn't long before Mom called us to put my stuff in the car. I had accumulated a small number of clothes, but no real earthly possessions, except for a pair of Wenchell's Donuts rainbow sunglasses that I wore while riding my scooter. I dropped them in the box I had already packed, and then there was no more avoiding the inevitable. With a heavy heart, I gave Carol and Ma a long hug and thanked them.

Carol squeezed me tight and whispered in my ear, "I love you, Joe."

We both wiped the tears from our eyes and she held my hand for one final embrace before letting go. I was now officially back in Mom's hands, following the rules, making sure I listened and was "good." She and her boyfriend took turns driving into the darkness. The next morning, we woke up on Aunt Darlene's doorstep, where she once again welcomed me into her home with a big smile and hugs.

Mary Jane Lane

Aunt Darlene lived in a 1970's mobile home in a large mobile home community on the outskirts of Glendale, AZ. Beyond the trailers were groves of orange trees that stretched their branches wide to connect to Sun City, a retirement community. Inside the home, the decor was a mix of shaggy brown carpet, yellowish countertops, an avocado green refrigerator with floral wallpaper on the front, and brown wood-paneled walls. We quickly settled into Aunt Darlene's house and the rhythms of school and church.

Mom's boyfriend was another short-lived relationship, but there was another one waiting to emerge from the revolving door of her endless line of men. After about a month, like the movie Groundhog's Day on repeat, Mom started telling us a familiar story. "I met someone," she began, "We're moving into a one-bedroom apartment that's fully furnished. There's a pullout couch for both of you to sleep on." Then, she added, "Or you can stay here with Darlene. She said it would be okay."

Trying to hold back tears, I slowly looked at Pat, trying to get a sense of what he wanted to do. Summer would be here in a few months and he would be off to the carnival, leaving me on my own wherever I ended up. Did I want to share a bed with him in Tom's dirty trailer for the summer, or risk it with Darlene? She had shown more concern in those several weeks than I had received from Mom in years. Pat's decision was clear, as were his feelings about Mom's constant game of 'Who's taking my kids this time?' I could read Pat's thoughts on his face, which was still staring Mom down:

"Fuck it, I'm staying here. What have I got to lose? It's better than any day with you."

I translated Pat's internal dialog, "We'll stay here with Aunt Darlene."

Mom nodded in agreement and began packing her things. It was so matter of fact; didn't she want to be with her kids? Did she love us? Did she even want us? She explained that we'd see her at church and that Darlene would be there to support us. If we needed anything, we could just call. We received the obligatory hug along with "listen and be good," and just like that, Mom was gone, again.

Darlene was a confident, single woman with long brown hair that she put in hot curls almost every day. She was direct, bold, followed most rules, loved horses, and was always looking for a good deal. She was a movie buff, especially rom-coms, and Patrick Swayze was her favorite actor. She loved movies so much that she built wooden shelves along the living room wall to store them all, and watching them became a pastime for friends when they came over. Pepsi was her drink of choice, even over water. When I could afford a beeper, she even figured out how to spell Pepsi with numbers to ask me to pick some up on the way home. She knew the amount of pain, neglect, and abandonment the children in my family had experienced and did her best to create a loving environment for us. Darlene took on the role of mom, dad, counselor, friend, and pastor. She sacrificed regularly to provide for me and my brother. If she had five dollars left in her pocket, she would give it to us instead of spending it on herself. She spoke of our potential while we were shrouded in the cloak of darkness that was our pain. Like Carol and Ma, I trusted Darlene quickly. Partly because she made me feel welcome in her home and she created space for me to feel the emotions of Mom leaving time after time. She didn't try to fix things, she just wanted us to know someone actually cared.

Similar to the Carnie Code, Darlene's rules came in threes: go to church whenever the doors are open, sing in the church choir, and don't break her trust. Her Church of Jesus was the same one we had attended when we lived down the street from the projects as small children. It was an unaffiliated Pentecostal church that focused on modesty and being "in the world but not of the world." Women had long hair and didn't wear pants to church, men's hair shouldn't touch their collar. Men were the rightful head of the house, and women were to submit to them. There were endless rules to follow to avoid being caught in 'Satan's snares,' which was helpful to me because I had found comfort in knowing the rules to avoid Mom's wrath. To be safe, all I had to do was "listen and be good."

Every Sunday morning, three retired fluffy-haired ladies, each with a different color; pink, blue, and white, would be at the church doors. They'd always give you a bulletin, and sometimes fashion advice – in other words: were your clothes appropriate for God's House. They were really kind souls and I welcomed their hugs. Pastor Outlaw was there to greet us with his big smile, half-crooked teeth, and a big hug. The small membership consisted mostly of single moms or retired women and was very white, except for our gay, black organist. Services were the same as when I was a little kid: two to three hours long, filled with fire and brimstone experiences and moments of the Holy Spirit 'coming down' on us. We were taught that if people didn't believe our way and follow our rules, they wouldn't join us in heaven. Between the Holy-Ghost-dancing, outdated and oppressive gender roles, speaking in tongues, hair length, and dress codes, we were pretty strange to the outside world. This made it difficult to have friendships outside the church. (You may be thinking, was this a cult? Although it was very rigid, inward-focused, and shame-driven, I don't think it was. It was a group of people who loved each other, loved God, and felt that if they followed the rules of the Bible and the pastor, they would go to heaven. Weird? Yes. A cult? No. A little crazy? Absolutely.)

In our church, it was more about modesty than what you wore. Women could wear pants, makeup, and jewelry – though not too much – and they could also cut their hair. I agreed with all the rules except one: men's hair should not touch their shirt collars. In short, if your hair was longer than that, you were acting feminine. I loved my hair in high school. I grew it out, cut it short, and had it permed twice. For me, it was a fun way to express myself. As soon as it got close to my collar, the fluffy-hairs would start saying something about getting a haircut. For once, I didn't care what they thought. I would reply, "Jesus had long hair." That usually stopped them from saying anything else.

Fashion was also a big thing for me. Though I didn't follow any trends, I went for 'classic with a flair.' Black pants and a white collared shirt seemed boring for church so I went shopping. The Oaktree store in the mall was my favorite. There, I could also get shirts with a banded collar, which pissed off the fluffy-hairs because it wasn't a real 'church shirt.' When I saw their reaction, I bought bolo ties to really freak them out. Anyway, it was my way of expressing myself. The younger Joey was saying, "Please look at me. See me. Appreciate me. Isn't my bolo tie cool?"

After three hours in church, you get pretty hungry. In the Pentecostal world, there were two main options for Sunday afternoon lunch. Option one: a buffet restaurant. We'd herd into the endless line of white church people and grandmas waiting to pay for endless amounts of buttered, overcooked vegetables, a meat fest carved by a human meat slicer in a white coat and hat, a simple salad bar, and endless amounts of mediocre desserts – Jell-O three ways, cake, pie, and ice cream. It was heaven on earth and everyone filled multiple plates like it was the Last Supper. Option two: a Mexican restaurant. We'd order cheesy plates of goodness that radiated so much heat that your face could get a sunburn. Even if the server said, "Hot plate," you'd still touch it and get burned. When the plate finally cooled, the iceberg lettuce would melt into the cheese, leaving soggy threads of mush to scoop up. Although our bellies were already overstuffed with chips and salsa, we still made room for our enchiladas, burritos, tacos, and tostadas.

Once our feast was done, we'd head home for a few hours of rest before returning to church for the evening. It would be another few hours of singing, preaching, and getting in trouble with the church deacon for talking too much or sitting too close to the opposite sex. After the service, we'd decide which Dollar Menu to consume to satisfy our adolescent appetites. Oh, the deliciousness of a nacho supreme, no green onions, a taco supreme, and a fountain Pepsi that always tasted better than the can. Wherever we went, we showed up an hour before closing with ten to fifteen hungry teenagers, with Aunt Darlene carting several of us. We were usually the only ones in the dining room, so they'd clean around us. We'd break up into groups of friends. Couples who had been chastised in church for being too close were now joined at the hips and holding hands under the table. We all joked about Pastor Outlaw's enthusiasm for heaven, his deep concern for those of us going to hell, and how he would yell from time to time to get the organist to hit some keys for some Holy Ghost-filled 'Amen.' The night would end with laughter, hugs, and lingering embraces before we'd see each other again at Wednesday's youth service.

The Hamack boys had an unspoken 'neutral zone' with anything church related. As we were different in so many other places besides church, this was where the two of us could find fellowship together. Pat had already made friends with the small youth group within the few months he stayed with Darlene. When I arrived, he was quick to introduce me. Pastor Outlaw's son and Darlene were in charge, and led us every Wednesday into the small chapel at the back of the church property. We would sing, and play silly games like stuffing as many balloons as possible into the pantyhose your neighbor was wearing over their clothes...and yes, we'd have plenty of time to study the Bible too. The evening would end with that favorite Pentecostal pastime – volleyball – and make-out sessions in the dark corners at the back of the main church building. On Friday nights, everyone would come to our house to watch one of the hundreds of movies Darlene had acquired and hang out on the front porch. Since the people in our church were pretty strange to the outside world, many of us relied on each other as our main group of friends. After years of packing, moving, then unpacking, changing schools, and trying to establish myself, I finally began to settle into a community that accepted (most of) who I was.

As the weeks since Mom had left turned into months, Darlene created a place where we could talk about anything. The endless tiny cuts of Mom's departure had the first signs of possible healing that served as a reminder not to let her get too close. She regularly asked us to visit her new place. I couldn't understand why we should go if she had made her decision to put another man ahead of her children. Darlene was clear, though: we still had to be respectful because she was our mom. The church taught us to respect our elders, even if they didn't respect us in return. Part of the belief was that children should listen, follow the rules, and obey. So, one day, with contempt in my heart for Mom, Pat and I got in the car with Darlene to be dropped off at her house for a few hours.

When we arrived, she was as happy as a lark, with the heart of a fifties housewife who took great care to clean the house and prepare sit-down meals for her guests. Her newly teased beehive welcomed us into the beige-covered room where her boyfriend was waiting, along with Sis and her son Erik. We ate lunch and then dressed to go swimming. Mom didn't know how to swim, and we were quite surprised when she suggested it. But then again, we were always surprised by her actions, so we went along. This was one of many times we had to act like a happy family in front of her boyfriend, who was sitting in a chair by the pool drinking a beer.

Sis sat on the side of the pool. It was one of the first times I saw her since she had returned to Tucson to be with David. She was now living in Phoenix, pregnant with her daughter Krista, and on the outs with the man that had beaten her and left me with a permanent knot in my left template. We exchanged a few pleasantries and continued to ignore the memory of the awkward goodbye that had occurred almost a year earlier. Time couldn't go fast enough before Darlene arrived to take us out of that awkward situation. As we drove home in silence, she asked how it went. We grumpily responded with indifference and joked about how Mom acted like we were a happy family. Both Pat and I had grown numb to Mom, knowing that she would choose a man over us any day of the week.

Since it was rare for all four of us kids to be together, when Pennie and Sis were in town for one of the carnivals, Pat and I wanted to go see them on a day when we had already planned to spend the night at a friend's house. When we asked Darlene if we could drive out to see our sisters, she made it clear that she didn't want us to go. Even though we knew that disobeying Darlene would be breaking one of her rules, we felt it was justified: it was to see our sisters after all! Pat had earned a reputation for not being very trustworthy, so I'd have to figure out how to convince Darlene we would stick to our original plan of staying with a friend. The excitement of doing something with our friends, with a dash of bad boy, got the best of me. I told Darlene, "Trust me, we're not going." She looked at me a little sideways and nodded in agreement.

YES!! It had worked! When Friday afternoon arrived, Jason picked us up. We grabbed some dinner, and headed across the valley in his brown 1980s camper shell truck. The carnival was full of energy and people. My sisters were working the food wagons, so I went over to say hi to them. I sat in the doorway while they worked, chatting about life, school, and the occasional Mom story.

In the middle of the conversation, I suddenly heard Darlene's voice, "Um, what are you doing here? Get home right now!"

I didn't say anything, there was no way to justify it. I got up, found the guys, and we left. Darlene had stayed in touch with Pennie over the years and had been planning to visit her, since Pat and I were staying with a friend. The thought that Darlene might go out to see Pennie hadn't even crossed my mind. It was an emotional ride home, sitting in the back of the truck, hoping that the shaggy brown carpet would make me feel better about breaking Darlene's trust. I knew we were in serious trouble.

When Darlene got home, she was still quite pissed off, though she never swore because of church rules. She did, however, say everything else that came to mind. "'Trust me,' you said. I didn't expect this from you, Joe!"

Her words hit my heart, then began to sink deep into my stomach. I had broken her trust. I went to my room in tears as the weight of what I had done set in. Darlene had been so quick to show love and care for me. Had I risked losing that for a stupid trip to a place I despised so much? Just to see my sisters? How could I make this right? We were grounded for a week, and that meant only school, church, and home. Lying to her was devastating, and she would remind me that I had broken her trust every time I used that word. It took me several years to earn it back.

Things between Pat and I were typical for two brothers who are a year apart. If Pat saw me walking down the hall at school, he'd make fun of me or bump into me to assert his dominance. I was okay with him being the alpha, but he wouldn't let other kids do it. He would step in to stand up for me, fulfilling the 'Carnie Code'. At home, however, we would go round and round pushing each other's buttons. I'd call him "Fat Pat" and he'd call me "faggot."

When Pat and I had bad days, we expressed our anger in different ways. On rare occasions, that would happen on the same day. Our aluminum-sided mobile home would explode with fiery breaths of swirling rage, stretching the walls like a balloon, then return to normal size as we exhaled whatever was left in the pits of our stomachs. Between fights, we'd fire off piercing words as our bodies remembered moves from seventh-grade wrestling practice to pin each other down. Darlene would step in to break us up, taking a few punches to the arm in the process. We didn't know how to control our pain, and we'd keep hitting until our senses came back to the room where Darlene was standing, ready to take the pain that we so desperately wanted to give away. She would send us to the corners of the living room and try to resolve the conflict.

One day after school, she called the two of us into the living room. As we sat on the couch she said, "If you're going to hit each other, the least I can do is protect you a little." Then she pulled out a pair of boxing gloves that she had bought at Wal-Mart. We immediately tried them on and took them for a test drive in the middle of the room. Over the next few weeks, we fought in the backyard in the overgrown grass. We would give each other a good beating, with a few angry words in between the punches. I'd tear up a bit if he hit too hard, and that would usually end the conflict. The gloves were much softer than the bare hands we had been using. Once we got rid of the energy that had been building up inside of us, Darlene was able to get to the bottom of what was really going on.

These bouts of punching each other in the backyard of a trailer park were some of the last moments Pat and I spent together living in the same house. We spent a total of nine months together at Darlene's. Nine months of church, volleyball, girlfriends, movie nights, and hanging out with friends. Nine months of the Hamack boys being in one place, together, under one roof. Now, all that was coming to an end. Pat wasn't a fan of going to school, so he decided to drop out. To him, life looked better while working than sitting in a classroom. He quickly found a job working for a friend at a used car dealership. Darlene was clear, though; if he wasn't going to school, he couldn't live with us. So he moved in with my sisters. He showed up at church occasionally, but it felt as if his new life separated him from the rest of the group. His presence faded over the next few months as he prepared for another summer at the carnival. This began his cycle of work for the next few years until he finally decided to join a larger carnival in California. Pat and I didn't see eye to eye often, especially about the carnival. But his being my protector, showing me how proud he was of me, and finding a safe place to feel loved and accepted –were truths we lived by. He found his new safe place at the carnival and I was happy for him.

I found my own happy place in an unlikely corner. Our small church rarely interacted with others, either because we were not part of their larger organizations or we were too strange for the mainstream. There was one exception, however. Because of Pastor Outlaw's South Phoenix roots, community involvement, and sheer likeability, he was known by smaller black gospel churches for his civil rights and equality efforts in low-income communities. Our all-white choir regularly traveled to South Phoenix to perform with them. These weren't competitions, just a community of churches coming together to raise their voices to the heavens. We stuck out like a sore thumb, and yet the other choirs were so welcoming: shaking hands, giving hugs, and scooting over to make room so we could sit with them in a pew. Most church choirs were transitioning to wearing the same color clothes, but we had the brilliant idea of wearing the shimmering purple polyester robes of the 1970s with a reversible silver or gold sash.

After spending weeks practicing two songs, our Sister Act moment was here, minus Whoopi. When the first choir was ready, the organist took the stage, followed by the choir director, but no choir. The director faced the audience, cued the organist, raised his hands, and with a clap the choir entered from the back of the room, stepping and swaying in sync.

Dressed all in black, their voices were the cries of an army confident of victory as they marched into battle, dripping with the sounds of generations of struggle and overcoming. They were not individual voices, but a sole organism, come to life. My eyes widened as the music poured into my ears, saturating my heart and soul. It came from a different place than I had ever experienced. I could hear their life story in the way they sang, how they moved together, and the dependence they had on a far greater God than I had ever known. It made my soul come alive.

I had listened to a lot of music growing up, but this was different. It spoke to the innermost parts of me. When I didn't have the words to express the torrent bubbling inside me, music seemed to do it for me. It gave me a new perspective on how the black community could tell the story of oppression, brutality, and resilience to become who they truly were. I know there is so much more to their story than I can even fathom, but it gave me a glimpse of their struggle, their hope, and their strong sense of community. It was comforting and made me feel accepted. For a full-fledged 'white boy,' I had a decent voice and knew how to clap in time and sway with the group. Our choir, even on our best day, could do neither. When this choir started singing, I couldn't help but jump to my feet to clap and sway with them. I was the only one in my choir to do so, but I didn't care. I wanted to join the community we were being welcomed into in this moment of reflection and celebration.

When it was our turn, we all lined up on the side stage and walked onto the stage, shimmering in our purple robes.

Pastor Outlaw thanked the churches for inviting us to be a part of the evening. He queued up our pianist and organist, then let out a screeching and began to sing. It took the audience a moment to get their bearings, then they were on their feet cheering us on, clapping, swaying, and celebrating in their own way. We sang a style of music, which was completely different from any of the other choirs. We didn't clap in time or sway in sync, and it didn't matter. We were part of a larger family raising our voices together. At the end of the night, we were hugged and kissed as "brothers and sisters." Still coming down from the adrenaline rush, we walked to the car in a sea of conversation about how it had been the best night of our lives, how we were grateful for being accepted by the other choirs, and how we hoped to do it again soon. Gospel music, and even the Gaither Choir, still hold a special place in my heart when I want to connect with God in a very personal way. It is half nostalgia and half nourishment for my spirit.

Darlene was far more than a generous person. She had allowed me to live in her home and paid for school clothes, Christmas gifts, birthday parties, graduation, and even car insurance into my early 20s. She was selfless and wanted to give me what I didn't have when I was younger. Her job as an office manager had taken care of the bills when it was just her, but now she had a child. She couldn't count on getting anything from Mom, so she figured out how to 'rob Peter to pay Paul,' several times over the years. Food boxes from the church filled some of the gaps, and she still seemed to make ends meet. Partly, I think, through faith and sheer willpower. If she really wanted to do something, she figured it out.

Road trips were an easy way to escape the heat of Phoenix summers. All it took was a tank of gas and a Taco Bell drive-through and we were off for a day trip to visit Pat at the nearby carnival or to cool off at Slide Rock in Sedona. If there was a chance to get out of town and Darlene had some extra money, we were gone. Though most trips didn't take us far, California was the place Darlene really wanted to be, because of the ocean and the San Diego Zoo. I think Six Flags California was the best vacation we ever had. Darlene saved her tax return and squirreled away any extra money she could so we could go on this trip.

When the day finally came to walk through the gates at Six Flags, my childhood memories moved from the back of my mind to center stage. When I was a kid on the carnival, my sisters would take me on a kiddie roller coaster and I hated every minute of it. Each time it did that little loop to go up and then down, I screamed in agony like my life was ending. Yes, I was that kid on most of the rides. My sisters laughed and held my hand, which was little comfort. I couldn't even handle a tiny little kiddie coaster. And now I was literally stepping up to the big leagues to spend the entire day riding in the Six Flags scream machines. These rides were definitely better maintained than the ones at the carnivals I grew up on, so I wasn't worried about safety. It was more the twists and turns, the spinning, and the upside-down that I wasn't really looking forward to.

As we stood in line for The Batman Coaster, I kept my emotions in check, partly excited that we were actually doing this and partly holding in my pee because I was so scared. We got on the ride, buckled up, and were off. There were so many drops, twists and loops that we couldn't stop laughing. Surprisingly, I was immediately hooked. Darlene and I were like two little kids enjoying the wonder of amusement at its finest. We ran – well walked fast – from ride to ride. We couldn't contain how much fun we were having on the last ride and didn't realize how loud we were until we saw that people in the next line were staring at us. But we didn't care. That day, I felt no pressure to worry about anything but having fun. As the sun faded into the glow of early evening, with the screams of children and adults echoing in the background as another roller coaster took a loop or twist, Darlene and I walked to the parking lot. Our adrenaline was slowly wearing off, leaving us with just enough energy to carry ourselves back to our hotel room.

The next day, we spent it at the beach, relaxing and taking in every moment. Darlene loved the sound of the waves, but she didn't care much for the water, probably because it was too complicated to find appropriate swimwear with her Pentecostal roots. In her not-so-distant past, women literally swam in dresses. She figured it out, though. Neither of us were too keen on swimming, it was more about just being on the beach. We found a place to spread out hotel towels and walked down to where the sand meets the ocean. Water squirted out of the sand with each step until I was firmly planted in the first few inches of the cold ocean. As wave after wave crashed, the force pushed me further into the sand, my feet rooted to the shore. I could feel the push and pull of the waves. I closed my eyes, took a deep breath, and listened to the sounds of the salty sea. The thunderous waves crashing in the distance, the cackling of birds searching for their next meal, and the laughter of little children filling another bucket for their sandcastle.

I was transported back to the Tucson desert, playing in the riverbed with my brother, feeling the first drops of the monsoon on my face and smelling creosote in the air. *"You're going to be okay, Joey. Enjoy this moment,"* I said to my younger self. The soothing breeze, the calming waves, and the soft sands settled my mind and allowed me to be fully present. I never made it to the San Diego Zoo with Darlene, but I did understand why the beach was a special place for her. Now, it was for me too. She had given me a moment to let go of what was happening in life and just be. I hadn't learned how to do that as a child out of sheer survival. As my body came back to the present and for the first time, the weight didn't feel as heavy.

Thorn

Even though I had friends at church, I didn't feel like I fit in. I wasn't into sports, cars, or any of the other normal guy stuff. Yes, I could talk about God and church stuff, but it seemed easy for the other guys and girls to interact together. Although I liked the idea of dating a girl, it was usually awkward for me. I chalked it up to not having a lot of experience and following the rules really well. I had kissed plenty of girls, going back to my kindergarten crush, Renee, but kissing still felt a little bit off. I wanted the fireworks and butterflies in the pit of my stomach but never seemed to find them. There was still this undercurrent when seeing an attractive guy, and that's where I did feel those butterflies. When I thought about it too much, being found out felt like a noose slowly tightening around my neck. The fluffy-haired ladies at church would turn into oversized bobble-heads, nodding in shame and wagging their fingers at me with all the fire that Pastor Outlaw poured out from the pulpit.

At church, if something kept you from following the rules or living the life God had 'called us' to live, it was sin. If this sin was a constant, like my struggle, it was considered a thorn in the flesh. I was so afraid of what my struggle meant for me. I just wanted to be loved and accepted for who I was. No conditions, no extra rules, no "I'll love you if..." Instead, I was constantly reminded that if I gave in to my sin, I would be separated from God and my community. It was all or nothing. I wasn't even sure if I was gay, but not having a place to talk about it reinforced that the only way to be safe was to hide it. This wasn't the life I wanted, and I asked God to take it away every day. I worked constantly to follow the rules better than everyone else, to read my Bible more, to show that I was a good Christian. If I did it well enough, dated a good Christian girl, and talked the talk, 'it' would surely go away; it had to.

After doing my best to follow all of the rules and "being good," as Mom would say, nothing ever changed. I felt isolated, lonely, and began to pull inward. The Bible telling me that God wasn't giving me more than I could handle seemed like a lie. Why would He allow this to happen to one of His creations? I despised who I was and became harsher with myself in order to push what was going on inside as far away as possible. The stress of it all began to affect my willingness to eat. Hell, it was one place I felt in control. Darlene noticed that I was losing weight quickly and realized something was wrong. She had been there for me so many times before. We really could talk about anything. But what about this? What would she think if I told her? Could I trust her? Would she stop loving me?

One night, after watching a movie with friends that had the slightest gay undertone, I worked up the courage to tell her. It wasn't that I was gay, I just found guys attractive. While I was sobbing on her bed, she made space for me to sit in the pain. She leaned over and rubbed my back, "I am so sorry this is happening to you. You kids have been through so much. I wish I could take it away from you." We sat in silence for a few minutes as I composed myself. "How can I help?" she asked as she hugged me. I wasn't sure what she could do or how to fix what was wrong with me. But for that night, just her being there was enough. It slowed the tightening of the noose, though that would inevitably return, along with the shame that I was broken and couldn't be fixed.

I had very few friends at school, so my friends at church were my community. Even though Sunday services were pretty weird, Wednesdays were a little more relaxed and people felt like they could invite friends. One of those friends was Todd. He was a ball of energy, comfortable in his own skin, ready to burst into song or terrible dance moves at any moment, and able to make most people feel welcomed from the moment they walked into the room. He was an attractive guy, so the ladies were excited to see the dating pool expanding. He was a year older than me and seemed to like similar things like music, singing, and hanging out with the girls.

Todd and I became fast friends and were inseparable. He'd pick me up in his little red Mazda truck and we'd drive across town between our houses. He had grown up listening to Bette Midler, Barbara Streisand, and Barry Manalo. I quickly learned the music on our long drives and within a few weeks, we were belting out ballads together. Much like my friend Matt from Tucson, it felt like Todd accepted me as I was. I didn't love sports, nor could I play them well. I couldn't talk shop about cars or all the girls I had dated. That didn't seem to matter, we could goof off or be in silence. Todd knew about my mom leaving me and how hard life was growing up. I didn't have to pretend to be someone else or put on a brave face.

I was shocked when he told me that his oldest brother was gay. I remember meeting him once. I was a scared, anxious teenager, afraid he would pick up on my struggle. He didn't, or at least he didn't say anything. He just seemed 'normal,' which was unexpected because 'they' were portrayed so differently in the church.

After meeting his brother, I wondered if I could tell Todd a little more about being attracted to guys. At least he'd have a sense of what it was like, because of his brother. So I decided to ask more about what it was like for his family. Todd shared that it was difficult at first, but his family loved him, so they figured it out. I wondered, "Hmmm, could I really share this? Would he tell anyone?"

I decided to be cautious and started by telling him about Mike and his partner in California. "It was like they really cared for each other. They weren't ashamed of it. It was just their life. I think they loved each other," I paused and held my breath, waiting to see how he would react.

"Yeah, probably."

Okay, that wasn't a bad answer. What else could I say to him?

In our church, the only thing we heard about sex was that if you did it, you were sinning and ruining your life. If you masturbated, you were giving in to the devil. You now had sin in your life, and you had better repent. As a teenager, I felt like I had an erection more often than I didn't. I was a pro at covering my crotch with a binder or jacket during passing periods in high school and figuring out the boxer shuffle. The crazy thing was, we couldn't talk about it. Our church taught it was shameful to talk about our bodies and all it caused was lustful thoughts. If you were a good Christian, you could resist temptation and stay pure.

Todd and I were two rambunctious teenagers with a lot of testosterone coursing through our veins. We'd randomly bump into each other or try to tackle each other and even get into wrestling matches in my living room. We had little personal space, it was just normal for us. We slept at each other's houses as much as we could. As we'd turn out the lights, we'd talk about the day, what our plans were for the weekend, and what girls we liked. The room would go quiet and then we'd start talking again. On top of my attraction-issues, I was freaking out that I was going to hell for masturbating and I really wanted to talk to Todd about it. I figured with the lights out and both of us about to fall asleep, the stakes were pretty low and I could write it off as a joke if I had to. I lay there for several minutes, wide awake.

Finally, I cleared my throat, "Hey, can I ask you something?"

"Sure."

"Um, do you masturbate?"

The long pause that followed got awkward for a moment. I scolded myself, "*Damn, I crossed a line. We're not supposed to talk about this*" Thankfully, my thoughts were interrupted,

"Yeah. You?"

I let out a breath, "Yeah. I thought I was the only one." We both laughed, acknowledging our unspoken similarities as teenagers and what was happening to our bodies.

Over the next few weeks, we had deeper conversations and even joked about how normal masturbation seemed even though the church called it sin. It was refreshing to finally hear what everyone was probably thinking. I still didn't want to risk sharing being attracted to guys, though; that was off-limits. I shoved it to the corner and tried to ignore it. That was until our conversations turned into something more. Another sleepover opened the door to more questions, curiosity, and a little experimenting. It felt different than with a girl. With Todd, it was comfortable; those fireworks I had been looking for were in full swing.

Outside of our bedrooms, we had to act like friends and nothing else. If we were caught or there was the slightest hint, we would be called out and condemned. We would have been put on the sacrificial table as an example of what happens when you give in to the devil's wiles. I wanted to be with Todd, to sit next to him and hold his hand, to know what it was like to kiss another boy, something that would never be possible in my world. Even though I wanted to continue exploring with Todd, I was constantly racked with guilt and shame. I knew I was breaking the rules, and the pressure of hiding it had become overwhelming. In my mind, we had given ourselves over to sin. I continued to hear the fluffy-hairs repeat there was sin in my life and Mom's voice condemning me for not listening or being good. The only way to return to God was to repent.

The shame of what I had been doing with Todd was now too much to bear. The only way I thought I could absolve my sin and be "good" again was to come clean. Fearing judgment and rejection, I decided to tell our close friends and Darlene. Without telling Todd first.

It was a terrible mistake.

He was furious with me, and rightly so. I had shared something deeply personal with our friends without his permission.

When I tried to explain why, he responded, "You ruined everything and embarrassed me. Why would you do that? I'm done. I can't be friends with you anymore." And he walked away, straight out of my life.

I had been so focused on myself, that I hadn't even considered how it would impact him. I had broken his trust. I had humiliated him. And he may have just been curious, it was something more for me, but just not ready to face it. I did not feel absolved of my sin, only that I had betrayed my best friend; someone who cared about me, and now bore the shame of what we had done.

After the loss of Todd's friendship, facing the consequences of my actions at church, and broken trust in other relationships, I began to isolate myself, falling deeper into depression, not eating, not cleaning up after myself at home, and barely engaging at church. Darlene tried to be supportive but saw me shutting down more and more. She tried to ask what was going on and how she could help, but I was so mad at myself about Todd and full of hatred at the thought of liking guys that I couldn't even communicate with her. As we finished lunch after church one Sunday, the tension was high.

She put down her fork. "I want to ask you a question," she said. "Are you taking advantage of me?" She went on to explain that she felt like I didn't care about anything anymore and was just using her as a place to live.

I thought about what she meant by the question. Had I worn out my welcome, had I done something wrong, had the Todd issue broken her trust again? I had no idea why she was asking me, but as I thought about what the expectations were in her house and "being good." I was seventeen, had no parents, a borderline eating disorder, was probably gay, and had ruined my relationship with my best friend. I don't know if I was taking advantage of her or just trying to find some stability in my life.

Yet, I answered, "Yes."

As we sat across from each other at our favorite Mexican restaurant with half-eaten red chili burritos, she replied, "Then I think you need to move out." As I laid in bed that night, the darkness of the room multiplied by what happened earlier in the day. A voice deep inside me said, *"You're so stupid. How could you ruin this? Mom was right, you are a 'piece of shit'. Now Darlene, the person that loved you the most doesn't even want you."*

The days that followed were emotionless transactions in the place I had called home for the past two years. Darlene's mobile home had become a haven for me, the longest I had lived in one place since Mom and Tom divorced. It was a real home, with food in the cupboards and clothes that weren't either from the thrift store or Pat's hand-me-downs. I had my own bed, hell, my own room. It was safe from abuse and constant berating, and now I was headed to the unknown and surely back on a couch somewhere.

With Mom in Tucson, the only place I could go was to Sis's house, which was a small two-bedroom, roach-infested shithole. The surfing began again as I settled in on her couch. The roaches were so bad, they literally covered the walls and were in everything, from your clothes to food that wasn't completely sealed. If you turned on a light, they would say, "What's up?" and go about their business. We were outnumbered by thousands and they knew it. They went where they wanted and when they wanted. It must have been worse for the kids – Krista, two, and Erik, four, along with Pennie's daughter Kori who was there most days. Sis did her best to find an affordable place for her and the kids, and it was gracious of her to allow me to stay with her. If she hadn't let me stay, I don't know where I would have ended up.

When my senior year started, Pennie, Kori and Pat also needed a place to live, so we found a new three-bedroom apartment. Moving day could not come fast enough. We fumigated everything before we moved to do our best not to bring any roaches to the next house. Sis, her two kids, and occasionally David, who was back into the picture, shared the master bedroom. Pat and I bunked up, while Pennie and Kori were in the room downstairs. With seven people and both Pennie's and Sis's boyfriends visiting regularly, there wasn't much room. I was living out of the two boxes I had packed at Darlene's house a few months earlier. It was chaotic, to say the least, and when Mom started visiting you had to add to the dynamic. As siblings, we got along pretty well, but Mom was the detonator for the emotional explosions that just tore us apart. Even with my adult sisters, Mom would constantly talk down to us, yell at us, and scream at the grandchildren. She was just the same as she'd been in my childhood.

The feeling of not being wanted by Mom and the constant unrest in Sis's house finally brought me to a breaking point and I left. I bounced around on a couple of couches and ended up with an older couple from church, Leon and Marge. They lived a simple lifestyle, were generous to those in need, like a teenage boy who needed a place to live, and followed all the Christian rules. Leon ran the traditional conservative Christian home as the man of the house. He regularly talked about two things: the Bible, and how extraordinary God was and how He could show up in someone's life. It gave me hope that life wouldn't be as bleak as I thought it would be, considering what was said to me growing up. Marge was like a sweet grandma, making breakfast, helping with the grandchildren, and giving me a hug when I left for school. They lived on the opposite side of North Phoenix from my high school so I had to get up early and ride the city bus to the other side of town to get to school. I found a job down the street from their house that I'd go to after school, then back home to sleep on the couch. I would catch a ride with them to church, then spend time with friends. It felt like living with my grandparents. I knew they cared about me, hell they wouldn't have let me stay with them if they didn't, but it wasn't an option to stay there long term. I was grateful they gave me a place to live and food to eat, but it felt like I was putting them out. Still beating myself up for what happened with Todd and Darlene months ago, there was no way Leon and Marge would put up with me if they found out.

When I returned to school from winter break, Darlene and I started talking again. She learned how much time I was putting into work and school, and the amount of travel I was doing to do it all. One Sunday, she asked if I wanted to grab some lunch after church, then could give me a ride home. We talked about what life had been like over the past several months, what I was beginning to understand about myself, and how my decisions impacted the people around me. By shutting down and not sharing what was truly happening, I had made it impossible for her to help me. With the promise of better communication, she offered to let me move back in. We agreed that I would pay a small amount of money to help with food, just to have some responsibility as I prepared to graduate from high school.

During my junior year, Stephanie and her best friend, Chris, had become close friends. We met in our church youth group. Stephanie was dating my brother, which made it a little weird at times. She was also friends with Todd and ultimately became the bridge to heal our friendship. I knew he needed space, so I kept my distance. When I shared with Stephanie what had happened and why Todd was so upset with me, she encouraged me to remain patient, telling me that he needed time to figure things out himself. One Sunday, he acknowledged me. I was shocked. It wasn't a warm welcome, just a "hello," but it was something. After several weeks, we finally sat down so I could formally apologize and acknowledge my huge mistake. He shared how I had humiliated him and that what happened was more about being curious than anything else. I respected that and was still facing my own internal battle, but we were able to put it behind us. It took some time, but Todd and I became friends again. Life was finally starting to normalize. I was back home with Darlene, Todd and I were friends again, and I was about to graduate from high school.

Mom knew graduation was coming up and wanted to be part of the celebration. That was the last thing I wanted. Why would I want someone who had left me several times to celebrate my graduation? I refused to release tickets for her to attend that day. Obviously, I was still pretty angry about everything that had happened, and too immature to see anything else. Graduation night would be a celebration with my closest friends, showing their pride in my accomplishment.

I didn't know what lay ahead after that day ended. I had no plans for college and knew the military wasn't for me. Life was just survival, a constant, 'just get to the end of this and then you'll be okay.' I had no hope there was anything worth pursuing after high school, so I didn't make a plan. I was just figuring it out as I went. It had gotten me this far.

Final Thoughts

Aunt Darlene and my church did their best to give me a place and make me feel part of a family, but this didn't replace the loss of my actual family being gone. I had learned to bury my pain from Mom's past abuse, Tom not being around, and being attracted to guys. The only thing I knew I could control at the time was food, so I ate enough just to function, and my body began to reflect how I felt inside. I wasn't just withering from abandonment, self-hatred, and depression, but I was slowly dying. I had begun to push the pain to a distant place, the desert of my childhood. I knew there was nothing out there, it was desolate. If I left it out there long enough, I was sure it would just die from the heat and the lack of water to nourish it. I didn't want those parts of me to thrive, to let them feel the restorative raindrops falling from the sky, to penetrate the dusty earth and reach down to strengthen their roots. Truly, I wanted them dead, and then they would be gone forever.

Part Three

Baby Daddy

Relationships with Mom and Tom hadn't improved after high school. There was still this undercurrent of hating myself, of not facing the pain of Mom leaving, Tom not being around, and not feeling like I fit in anywhere.

As I was catching up with Mom's old friend, Nonnie, at a party she threw, she asked the basic questions about my family, school, work, etc. Then, surprisingly, she asked about Tom. I gave my usual answer: that I didn't really want to see him and that it had been almost a year since the last time. Nonnie, in her snap-up moo-moo and tightly permed gray hair, leaned toward me, indicating that she had some gossip to share. With her lit cigarette still hanging from her mouth, she said quietly, "Well, you know... Tom really isn't your dad." I paused, looked back at her, and nodded, signaling her to share more as I processed what the hell she was saying. I thought, *"Whoa, you're just going to throw that on the table without any precursor?"* Nonnie always knew the juicy details of everyone's life. People felt comfortable just hanging out while she was crocheting or cooking. They would pour out what was going on in their lives, so Nonnie was the keeper of secrets, or maybe just embellished gossip. Either way, she was the one to talk to if you wanted the backstory on something. She quickly realized that this was the first time I had heard this information. She retreated a bit and ended by saying, "It doesn't matter, any other guy wouldn't be much better."

Later that week, I called Pennie and told her what Nonnie said. She confirmed that it was probably true, and that she and Sis had known since they were young. This made me even angrier at Mom and a little upset at my sisters, knowing that they had been sitting on this huge part of my story, but had chosen to withhold it. A few names were thrown around, and it all confirmed Nonnie's original comments that these guys were not much better than Tom.

After talking to several people, I felt it was time to ask Mom directly. As Mom and I stood on the porch of my sister's apartment, my heart raced and my palms sweating profusely, but I didn't beat around the bush. "Is Tom really my dad?" I asked.

"Of course, why?" she replied.

I went on to explain what I had heard from Nonnie and the confirmation from others. She looked away.

"Yes, he's your dad," she replied again nervously. I wasn't sure if she was angry or upset. I tried to ask why people were telling me he wasn't and pressed the issue with more detailed questions, but she just replied, "I don't remember."

I was frustrated, and now she was crying, showing her embarrassment. It was hard to believe her. We had grown up watching Mom manipulate the system to get what she wanted or needed, and that included on many occasions, lying to get out of trouble. "I did my best for you kids, and that's it," she said. Then she walked away. I knew that was all I was going to get from her, so I decided not to push any further.

As though on a newly assigned Hardy Boy case, I began my investigation with friends who had known our family at the time, and they all confirmed the possibility. There was one person who kept floating to the top of everyone's list, John.

He had met Mom and Tom while working at the carnival and then spent some time at our house when I was in elementary school. John hadn't stayed in the house, though. He had built a makeshift fort out of old wooden pallets and plywood against the side of the house in the backyard. He was just another quirky guy – nomadic, quiet, with little focus in his life. What I do remember about John is that, like Nonnie had said, he wouldn't have made a better dad than Tom.

The timeline was a little vague, but goes something like this: Mom separated or possibly divorced Tom around the time Pat was born in Phoenix. Not one to be without a man, she quickly found the comfort of the next guy who would pay attention to her. Mom and Tom eventually got back together and she realized she was pregnant with me. Whether it's actually John or someone else, I'll never really know.

I knew there was one last person I could ask: Tom. It had been years since I had seen him. He still lived across town and was connected to Pat, but would he know anything? Was it even okay to ask? I considered the decision carefully, weighing the odds and whether I could even get the truth from him. Would I be opening an old wound, did he even know about John? But I couldn't bring myself to ask the questions. It would mean I'd have to rebuild my relationship with Tom, something I had avoided for years because of what he had done to my sisters. Emotionally, I couldn't handle the thought of what it would require of me, so I never asked him those questions.

I tried to move on, but struggled with the internal conversations, *"I'll be fine. I don't need a dad. I've made it this far. I clearly don't need a mom; she's proven that."* Over the next few months, trying to find my place in the world and processing the lie of Tom being my dad, I began to ask myself bigger questions, such as: What does it mean to be a man? Is there even a healthy example of one? Is this all life is going to be for me? Above all, the feeling kept following me that I had to be good but I would never be good enough. Life was going well, I had a steady job, a solid group of friends, and I had started graphic design school. But I still felt lost, lonely, and abandoned. I could be in the middle of any of these places and the waves of emotions would crash over me as I tried to tread in the abyss of my pain and shame. I was sinking fast, and thoughts of suicide set in. If my parents didn't want me, if I couldn't run away from the thought of being attracted to men, then how could I "be good" like Mom wanted me to be? I wasn't worthy of being loved, so how could I love in return?

I had seen some news stories about people overdosing on over-the-counter medications, and began to wonder if this was the answer. I had tried everything I thought could solve the problem. I prayed for years, asking God to take away the pain of not being wanted. I assumed that if anyone cared, He would, but that didn't seem to be the reality. I was desperate to feel better, to stop hating myself, to be loved and comforted by a mom or dad that had the capacity to. *Kneel down to my level, look me in the eyes and say I love you Joey. Hold my hand and tell me you're proud of who I am,* was that too hard to ask? Maybe taking these pills would finally solve the problem. It was a very loose plan, but it was all I could muster. The anguish of holding all of it in was too much to bear and I couldn't live like this anymore.

As Friday night came, Todd, his girlfriend Allison and her mom, and Stephanie had asked me to go to a concert in downtown Glendale. Listening to Christian music had become a staple for all of us, and one of our friends was hosting the event. It was the last thing I wanted to do, but Stephanie said she would drive over and drag me out of the house if it came to that. I reluctantly said yes. Everyone met at my house, and we drove over from there. I don't remember much of the concert, it just provided background music as I went over the plan for what was going to happen later that weekend. We walked back to my car while everyone chatted about the concert and made plans to go out for dinner. When I pulled out my keys to unlock the car, I noticed a card on the windshield. Assuming it was an ad for a local restaurant, I was going to just throw it on the ground, but I turned it over instead. It wasn't an ad for tacos, it was a Bible verse. Jeremiah 29:11 – "For I know the plans I have for you, plans to give you hope and a future."

I was stunned and stood there for a moment to clear the fog that had settled in my mind. I looked around as if someone was playing a joke on me. I walked up and down the street looking for other cars with a card on their windshield. My friends asked me what I was doing, but I was too focused on getting answers to respond. I ignored them and ran across the street to check the windshields, expecting to see another card. But it was just my car. My heart and thoughts began to race, *Why? Who would put this on my car? How could they know what I was going to do?* Allison's mom and Stephanie kept pressing me to tell them what was wrong. Their voices were muffled as I tried to understand what this meant. I quickly pulled myself together as everyone waited for me to unlock the doors. I shoved the card deep into my pocket and said, "Nothing, just some stupid ad," then got in the car.

As I pulled out of my parking space, pressing against my leg I felt a heat where I knew the card was stuffed in the bottom of my pocket. A voice inside told me, "Hey, I got this. I see you. There's more to life than what's happening right now. I will be your dad and I will never leave you." As I became overwhelmed with emotion, the inner pain I had been carrying began to pour down my face. I couldn't drive another moment and pulled over. We sat in the car as I made my way to the surface from the dark abyss that had overtaken my life. I told them what I had planned to do that weekend. I had been looking for a lifeboat, but everything seemed to pass me by as the waves pushed me further under the surface of the ocean. This card was my lifeboat. I'd thought God had gone silent and didn't care, wouldn't help. But He really got my attention. We spent some time talking about what was going on. They shared how sad they were that I couldn't share it with them and vowed to support me in getting help.

Life didn't get better overnight. It took months of holding on to the idea that God really cared, my friends showing up regularly, and finding a therapist. I put the card on the mirror in my bathroom to remind myself every morning that I wasn't alone. I desperately wanted to feel loved and I didn't have anything else to hold on to, so it was pretty easy to accept what I felt God was telling me. Yet, if He was saying that He would be my dad and I would be His son, I still had to answer the questions I had been pondering. *What does it mean to be a man? Who in my life is healthy? Can I be different from my own family? Is this all life is going to be for me? I'll never be good enough.* But now there might be answers. If I was God's son, then I didn't have to carry the weight of my childhood. I could be a healthy man, I could write a new story for my life; the cycle of neglect, abandonment, and abuse could be broken, and I could be a loving husband and dad. And it didn't take long for me to decide that to canonize this experience and begin to create something new, my first step would be to change my name.

My first step to figure out who I wanted to be meant I had to deal with my childhood. That required months of therapy to begin the healing process. After beating the crap out of a chair with a plastic baseball bat, journaling those things I didn't want to say out loud, and visualizing Jesus next to a stream to accept His love, I slowly began to realize that these were things that happened to me, not who I was. I didn't want to be remembered for my sad childhood, but for who I was in spite of it. A new name would be a new beginning, a way to look forward. Something to represent what I stand for, who I am, and to tell the story of how I lived my life.

There's a difference between thinking about change and actually doing it – whether it's changing your hair, your physique, or your name. I had figured out the why, but the how was a little more difficult. What would changing my name actually do for me? If it was to no longer be a Hamack and distance myself from my family, that wasn't a good enough reason. I no longer wanted to be the kid with no parents. When someone heard my last name, they would smile and feel honored for knowing me because I learned from them and they were encouraged by me. Okay, now I am getting somewhere. Now, was there anyone who could help with something like this? How do I even choose a name?

Midweek, I need to do one of the mundane tasks of being an adult, paying bills. On my lunch break, I ran to the Hallmark store in the mall where there was a post office in the back. As I was waiting, I looked down and saw two boxes with "Do It Yourself Legal" printed on them. One was for filing for divorce and the other was for changing your name, all for the low, low price of twenty-five dollars. I thought it was a joke, like a pet license you could buy a few doors down at Spencer's. But I was intrigued. Could it really be real? I bought one and took it home. The packet had about ten pages of questions as basic as "Why are you changing your name?" to determine if you were avoiding outstanding debts or the law. I decided to fill them out and see what happened. A small stack of papers stood between me and the person I wanted to become.

Before I could fill out that last form, I had to come up with a new last name. I started with common ones like Williams, Smith, Olsen, and even my pastor's last name, Outlaw. Nothing seemed to fit. I knew I wanted to keep part of the name "Hamack" to honor who I used to be and went through several iterations. The "mak" part felt comfortable but too short. Then I started adding endings, mak-stone, and too many letters. Mak-stein, I wasn't Jewish. Mak-ston, maybe. For the next week, like a junior high school girl pining for her new crush, I practiced writing Joseph Makston, Joseph Matthew Makston, Joe M Makston, and Joe Makston – minus the hearts and squiggly lines. It was settled. I filled out the final form and was ready for my day in court.

The day arrived when I would stand before a judge to start the next phase of my life. This was a big deal and I asked Darlene to go to the courthouse with me. We sat in the courtroom with six or seven other people who had come to do the same thing. The judge came in and addressed all of us at the same time.

"Good morning. I understand you are all here to change your names. I'm going to say this once, so please listen. When I'm finished, I'll call the first person." He gave instructions to step forward, hand your paperwork to the bailiff, state your current name, and explain why you're changing it. He'd ask the same questions that were on the form, then what your new name would be. The two people before me had emigrated from other countries and were Americanizing their names because they were too long or difficult to pronounce.

Finally, it was my turn. I looked at Darlene and smiled, took a deep breath, and walked up to talk to the judge. He asked me why I was changing my name. I explained that I had found out that the man I thought was my dad wasn't and that I had spent the last two years trying to find out who it was, but without success. I decided it was a chance to become who I thought I was supposed to be. He nodded in agreement, asked the rest of the standard questions, stamped the form, and said, "Okay, as of today, you are legally Joseph Matthew Makston. Have a good day, son." At that moment, I felt free. I no longer lived under the shadow of the history that came with my former name. I could now determine who Joe Makston was going to be, what he stood for, and how I wanted to be remembered.

Changing my name set me on a path of discovery. I could really be anyone, I could define myself and my family name. Now, I could start to build for myself. I could take the parts of my family that made sense to me and rebuild them for this new life.

Transitions

Have you ever seen the desert in the spring? For months, plants have survived on little rain, which only dampened the ground and barely nourished their roots. Then, as February gives way to March, the light rains soak deep and ignite new growth. The barren land and hills, once painted in muted shades of gray and brown, give birth to a rainbow of wildflowers that blanket the ground. As the sun rises, the cacti proudly display their magenta, white, yellow, and orange flowers, thanking the rain for the gift of new life. That's what it was like to go from Hamack to Makston.

The barren landscape that had driven me to consider suicide began to change as my friends supported me and I sought therapy. I realized that I could give more than I was given, that I could be better than my parents' examples. I could live a life that gave me fulfillment instead of limiting it to the four walls of a church in north Phoenix. Being Joe Makston gave me hope, a smile on my face, and a new direction in life on my terms. I held my head a little higher and maybe I had a little swagger in my step – but probably not, I wasn't that cool. I began to see relationships, my own judgments, bad habits, and parts of my community that were downright unhealthy and others had just changed. I didn't really know what it meant to be this new person with a new name, or how to represent myself – that would really take a few more decades to really understand. For now, I knew my roots were strengthened and the landscape began to change.

Following the rules and being good were still embedded in me, but the formality of it didn't give space to ask questions or suggest change. No, we had to live under the guidance of decade old rules, isolation, and shame. I realized it was time to leave my church home and fluffy hairs to find one that fit me a little better. My friend Stephanie's family had recently moved to a church not too far away, and I decided to join them. That is where I met Russ and Joy, who were the youth pastors. The church was pastored by Joy's parents and was twice as charismatic as my previous one. It had adopted a prosperity mindset from a Christian television network called TBN. My previous church felt that it was honorable to live a humble life and barely make ends meet, this increased our faith in God. This new church believed that God wanted to bless us abundantly, to give us a 'double portion,' and that He wanted to bless us ten, fifty, and a hundred times over because we could never 'outgive' God. I was totally on board with this thinking. I had lived with the bare minimum for so long. If I gave a little more to the church for God's work, I could finally reap the rewards. So, I basically went from one crazy group to another. It wasn't a bad fellowship at all. I actually felt better about myself and was encouraged by it. However, as with anything, if you do it too much it will just get weird.

Russ, his wife Joy, and Stephanie were the silver linings for me. We quickly became friends because we were the only twenty-somethings in the church. We relied on each other and hung out together most days. Russ and Joy had three kids, so it felt like being back with my sisters and their kids. There was a lot of life, energy, and laughter in their home. As I spent more time with them, we got to know each other's stories. They had been the popular kids in high school, had a teenage pregnancy, got married young, and started serving in Joy's parents' church. In turn, they learned about my mom leaving me, not knowing my dad, growing up at the carnival, and changing my name. They were shocked by my story, having assumed that I must have had wonderfully loving parents growing up. I thanked them for the compliment and for seeing who I was despite my upbringing.

Joy could sense that I had unresolved anger toward my mom. Even after several months of therapy, it was still difficult to even think about having a conversation with her, knowing how easy it was for her to leave her children with someone else. It was a Sunday afternoon, church and lunch were over, and we were back at their house, hanging out for the afternoon. Joy had started asking questions about Mom: where she lived, whether I was trying to talk to her, and what she might be doing for Christmas, which was coming up in a few weeks. I had no idea about any of this since I hadn't talked to her in so long.

Joy continued to nudge me. "Maybe you should send her a Christmas card," she suggested.

"Why on earth would I do that?" I said with a laugh.

"It would be a simple peace offering. Just let her know you're thinking of her."

I resisted any further conversation and said I'd think about it during the week.

A few days later, I was at the grocery store and what did I see? You guessed it: Christmas cards. The Hallmark aisles of hugs, comfort, congratulations, sympathy, and celebration all boiled down to a neat row of folded pieces of paper. *"Damn it, Joy was right. It is just a card. Maybe this will help. All right, let's do this."* I read card after card wishing the recipient peace in their holiday season, joy and comfort as they celebrate the birth of Christ. Hallmark doesn't make a card that says, "Thank you for abandoning me and my siblings several times. I'm not messed up at all. Merry Freaking Christmas!" I settled for the next best thing, grabbing a simple card that said, "Merry Christmas." I scribbled, "Hope you have a good Christmas" on the card and mailed it. Not expecting any response, I was perplexed to receive a birthday card in return. Written inside, "Thanks for the Christmas card. Happy birthday. Love, Mom."

When I told Joy and Russ, they continued to encourage me to reach out. The card turned into a phone call, which turned into dinner, and that changed everything. Joy's prompting and Russ's willingness to listen through my pain were the catalysts to accepting Mom for who she was, not who I hoped she would be. *"Maybe there were reasons why she left. I knew she didn't have a good home life, could that have impacted her ability to raise us?"* Choosing to think positively about the situation and say the best about her challenged me to my core. Which allowed me to see that she was trying to do the best with what she had. Therapy helped me identify what needed to heal. Time with Russ and Joy gave me space to experience the peaks and valleys of it. Part of me felt like I was giving Mom a pass on leaving, saying it was ok that she beat and berated us. The other part hoped we could have a relationship. The anger subsided enough to give way to grace. It was what I hoped God would give me in my pain. That He would show mercy in my weakness so I could feel loved. I wasn't sure I could do it with Mom, but I wanted to try.

Russ and Joy decided to start a new chapter in their family and moved to Seattle. Stephanie was in a relationship and about to have a baby. Meanwhile, I had become the senior pastor's right-hand man. It was a glorified role of security, secretary, and gopher. I stood outside his office door to greet people who wanted to see him, gathered him up to go to the auditorium for the service, carried his Bible and notes, and sat next to him in the front row. If he needed anything during the service, I would get it for him, whether it was water or telling the sound crew to turn the volume up or down. Being friends with Russ and Joy and having this position gave me access to the inner circle. I would speak during the offering to reinforce the 'double portion' philosophy and call out when people had just received one. As long as you towed the line and didn't challenge the pastors on their philosophy, things were fine. This became a problem, however, when Russ and Joy moved.

Now, I was one of two twenty-somethings in the church, the other being a quiet accountant who was so shy she could barely look at me to say hello. I wanted to meet other singles my age, so I decided to attend another church that had a Tuesday night singles group. When I arrived at the church that Wednesday night, everything was business as usual. I stood outside the pastor's door, sat next to him during the service, and walked with him to his office when the service was over. As I was leaving, he stopped me.

"Joe, I heard you visited another church," he said as he packed his things to go home.

"Yeah, it's hard to meet people my age here and I'd like to start dating." I replied.

"Well, don't you think God can bring the person you're supposed to be with here? It seems like you don't trust Him enough." He stopped packing his bag and turned to look at me. "If you go to another church looking for a wife, you're out of God's will and He won't bless it."

We went back and forth for a few minutes, while I tried to explain that I wasn't trying to leave the church, but I was lonely, needed friends, and wanted to meet someone to share a life with.

"You're wrong not to trust God here. He will not give you what you want in another church. Your faith is weak," the pastor said coarsely, then finished putting things in his bag and sat down at his desk.

As I stood there for a moment, my mind became clear, *Makston's stand up for themselves.* "No, you're wrong," rose from my gut, through my vocal chords, and into the ether. I took my church keys out of my pocket, put them on his desk and said, "Okay, I'm out." Then, I walked out of his office. I didn't wait for him to respond, I just walked out, got in my car and drove home.

With the headlights of other cars splashing in my face, I felt numb. *Did this conversation really just happen? Was I really out of God's will because I went to another church to meet people my own age?* It was absurd of me to think that. Until then, I had been naive to the fact that I was just following someone else's lead. The church had served as my family, a place of safety and love, but that only went as far as following its rules and living life its way. To my surprise, something deep inside me knew that what the pastor was saying was wrong and that it wasn't okay to stay there. It was hard to say goodbye to the people, but not to the pressure of living up to false expectations and outright manipulation. I was proud to stand up for myself. Joe Makston had begun to build the confidence to know when something wasn't right. I didn't want to be mistreated, and I knew there was more out there for me.

Finding another church home was harder than I expected. I was living in this charismatic subculture that made it difficult to relate to people in the real world. I had isolated myself so much that I didn't have any friends outside of the church, so I bounced around a few churches for several months. Some were even more strict than my previous two combined, and others just felt empty. I was frustrated and sad that I couldn't find my own community. One Sunday, I got up and got dressed for church. I had no idea where I was going, but I was raised to 'neglect not the assembling of the brethren,' which basically means: you better go to church every Sunday or God will hate you even more than He already does. This level of expectation and rule-following had determined my identity for decades. If I followed them, did what I was told, and was 'good,' as Mom always said, then I would be loved and accepted. Now, I started to think that was not really the case. If that were true, I would have a church, friends, and a wife to love.

Annoyed with myself, struggling back and forth, feeling lost, embarrassed, and alone, I drove up the freeway to the normal exit I would take to go to my old church. As I turned on my blinker and looked over my right shoulder to exit, I noticed another church building on the frontage road. When I approached the stoplight, I could turn left and go back to my old church or turn right and try this new place. *It's one more week, what have you got to lose Joe.* I unconsciously flipped on my right turn signal and followed the side streets back to the church parking lot.

The shit show, known as life so far, came with a sidecar of anxiety in new situations. Overwhelmed by the number of cars in the parking lot and the people entering the building, I sat in the truck for a minute. I was back on the kiddy roller coaster with my sisters, feeling every up, down and corner of the ride. But my gut told me, *You can do this, Joe. There are so many people, no one will notice you.* Trying to have a better perspective on life, I took a deep breath and went in. That was the first start of my many years at New Hope Fellowship.

As a kid, there were three places that felt safe and welcoming every time. My best friend, Matt's house, Charles and Noneen's, they were old friends of Tom's, and church. That's how I felt from the first moment I walked into New Hope that Sunday morning. It checked all the boxes of what I was looking for and then some. There were plenty of people my age, the teaching was good, I felt comfortable in the space, and the music was like listening to Christian radio. I had never heard that kind of music in a church before it was kind of... good!

The first few weeks were a bit like Disneyland, there was so much to do that I couldn't decide what to do first. There was a board in the lobby with flyers for 'small groups' that you could join, based on your life stage or interests. So I decided to divide and conquer: I'd go to the Sunday morning service and try the college group. Even though I was just over the average age of a college student, the group was the best fit for me.

That same week, I drove to the leader's house and sat in my truck for a few minutes. I was early, as usual. As I sat there, other people began to arrive. I needed to give myself a pep talk. *"This is it, Joe, you've got to get out of the car,"* I said to myself. My heart started racing and my stomach started to churn. *"What if it's like the last church? What if no one wants to talk to me? Then I'm stuck here."* I sat there a few minutes too long, now I was just a weird guy watching people go into a house. I pulled the car door latch and forced myself to get out. A few people said "hi" as I walked up to the house. They introduced themselves and walked right in without knocking.

The group leaders, Chris and Deana Marie, were there to greet everyone and introduce themselves to me. They offered me snacks, asked a few questions, and then introduced me to some other people who had arrived. That night was a bit of a blur, everything happened in double time. Someone played the guitar, and we sang; Chris shared from the Bible; and we broke into smaller groups to talk and pray together. It was almost magical. Twelve college students decided to drive to the far north part of Phoenix on a Tuesday night to spend time together. It was beautiful, comforting, and real. Yes, this was home. These were people I wanted to get to know, and hopefully, they wanted to get to know me.

A few months after I joined the group, another guy named Bret also joined. Bret had this innate ability to make me laugh at the drop of a hat. He'd laugh so hard that he'd wheeze from his asthma. As a child and teenager, I had hardly even been just silly. Maybe I took myself too seriously, maybe I didn't learn those skills, or maybe I was so traumatized that I never felt safe to be that free. Whatever the reason, around Bret, I felt free to be a dumb, free to be Joe. The first time we hung out at Bret's parents' house, we all went out to jump on the trampoline. Two of us got on, I took three jumps then my feet went right through the trampoline, ripping a hole in the middle. As I stood there, embarrassed and worried that this new friend and his parents would be upset with me, Bret just laughed hysterically. His dad still reminds me of that to this day, twenty years later. We'd hang out with the rest of the small group of friends, usually at someone's apartment or Bret's parents' house. We'd stay up way past what my 'rule-following' personality would allow, make late-night runs to Del Taco, play guitar, sing, have shopping cart races in empty parking lots, and pile up on a couch with everyone else to watch taped episodes of Small ville and Friends. We also talked about the important things: what was going on in our families, at work or school, what we were struggling with, and how we could support each other.

The idea of a group of people who love Jesus, coming together on a weekly basis and really doing life together wasn't foreign to me. However, the authenticity and vulnerability was entirely different from what I was used to. In high school I was taught that we were sinners and we couldn't get out of it. God was punishing us and we had to prove that we were good enough to get into heaven. If we did one thing wrong, we could spend eternity in hell. The next church taught that if I gave enough, He would give me everything I wanted in life. I did not realize until it was too late that the offerings went into the pockets of the pastors and not into the 'work of the Lord.'

New Hope was something completely new, a strange world of good music, relatable sermons, and a welcoming environment. It was literally the first church where I heard, "God loves you. Every part of who you are. Even the things you don't like about yourself." It took a few times of hearing that for it to sink in. It wasn't just some fluffy words the pastor said, there might be something to it. That's when the sirens and red lights went off in my brain. *RED ALERT, RED ALERT! NEW INFORMATION NEEDS TO BE PROCESSED!* It was as if my thoughts about God and church had done a Ctrl, Alt, Delete to reboot my way of thinking. *"Wait, pause, what? He doesn't hate me? He doesn't think I'm a piece of crap who's a constant annoyance? How is that possible? Is this a different God than the one I grew up with?"*

Even after letting go of the inner beliefs and stories I had written about who God was, I didn't think I could untie the bigger knots. My attraction to men was still showing up regularly. However, I decided to let it sit in that desolate place in the back of my mind, far enough away that I didn't have to think about it too often. Still hoping it would die. If I could do that, then maybe I could get away from the thoughts and find a woman who would love me. My new group of friends from church made it easier to move further and further away from it and focus on the 'right thing' of finding a wife and living out my responsibility to be a good Christian. The time we invested in each other, by having meaningful conversations and encouraging each other, led me to know that this was what I really wanted. Yes, this was what I was looking for; these were the friendships I wanted to cultivate. And maybe, just maybe, there was a woman out there who wanted that kind of relationship too.

Boy Meets Girl

My evenings and weekends were quickly filled with plans to hang out with my new friends. Christians and coffeehouses were a 'thing,' and we went to a lot of them. We'd drive around Phoenix to sparsely populated establishments and listen to our friend or a friend of a friend play guitar and sing... well, you get the idea. I'd order a chai tea latte and sit with everyone else to catch up on what had happened since the last time we saw each other. Between songs and sets, we'd share how God was speaking to us, what we were learning from studying the Scriptures, and how we were being challenged to live out God's plan. Everywhere we went, we'd meet a few more people from the larger group who were doing the same thing. Since I was the new guy, we'd do a round of introductions. My brain quickly compiled a roster with all the new names I had to remember, who might become a friend and even a potential date.

On Friday nights, Mill Ave, near Arizona State University, was one of our regular spots. There were a lot of mediocre restaurants and of course a coffee shop where a friend was playing a twenty-minute set. We all piled into cars and made the thirty-minute drive to Tempe to find our way to Coffee Plantation. A whiff of coffee wafted past our faces, as we entered the cramped shop. With our sugary drinks in hand, we grabbed a couple of tables and settled in. With a speaker five feet from our faces, we listened quietly as friends sang stories of love, brokenness, and hope in Jesus. As soon as they finished, we'd cheer and whistle to encourage them.

When the set ended, we were ready to walk through the college scene that brought Mill Ave to life. The smell of weed permeated the crowded streets. The bars and nightclubs spilled out onto the sidewalk as more students waited to join the fun. We were a little too 'Christian' to go to a place like that. A few 'starving students' would play their guitar on the street corner and there was the occasional megaphone evangelist. I never understood how they thought they were going to influence anyone... it always felt annoying and shame-filled.

Kara, one of the women in the group, said, "Oh, Nina is down here and wanted to meet. Let's go find her."

We wandered around for a while and completed a full loop back to Coffee Plantation. As we stood there, I wondered, *Why are we waiting for this person?*

Kara finally called Nina to describe where we were before suddenly calling out, "There you are! Look to your right. I'm waving at you." Kara hung up as Nina walked over. Kara smiled and said, "I forgot she had a date."

The little voice in my head tried to reconcile what was happening, "Really...? We've been waiting for someone who has a date to hang out with? What is going on?" I was a little annoyed.

As Nina approached us, everyone who knew her was already waving and ready to hug her. Then, I finally caught a glimpse of her. Everything went into slow motion, like in a movie. You know, when the guys see a girl that entices them and they make eye contact? All the surrounding noise goes silent, the person is backlit, and everyone else in the scene is blurred out. Her hair bounces as she takes each step, she smiles and makes eye contact with you. Yeah...that's what happened. *"Well,*

well, maybe she was worth waiting for," I thought. She had shoulder-length brown hair, wore tennis shoes, and a twin baseball jersey that was a little too short. Kara's introduction stopped the slow-motion movie sequence, and Nina reached out to shake my hand. Her bright smile and blue eyes still had me mesmerized as I tried to pull myself together and say "hello" back to her. She introduced her date, and I shook his hand as well. We talked to Nina and her date for a few minutes, catching them up on our plans for the evening, and then we were ready to go. As they walked away, I called out, "Nice to meet you." Nina echoed the same and disappeared into the crowded streets.

I stood there for a moment. "*Whoa, who was that woman? She's beautiful,*" I thought. Once again, Kara's voice pulled me out of my personal screening.

"Joe, I think we're going out. Are you ready?"

I nodded and gathered myself. As we got back into the car, I couldn't stop thinking about Nina. *What's her story? Is this guy her boyfriend?* Question after question popped into my head. As I buckled myself into the backseat, I mustered up the confidence to ask the question. "So what's the story with Nina? Do you hang out with her a lot?"

Sitting in the passenger's seat, Kara half-laughed and said with a slight tone of annoyance in her voice, "Don't date her, Joe. She'll break your heart." I would come to appreciate Kara's directness over the next few years and even thank her for saying those exact words over a decade later.

"Ah, no! I was just wondering because I haven't seen her anywhere else. That's all. She's clearly dating someone." I tried to brush off my question as pure curiosity. But I'm sure I wasn't very successful.

We rarely went to Denny's after an activity, but we were in a different part of town that night and there weren't many options. So, our large group walked in, and we sat down. To my surprise, Nina joined us from another event she had been attending. She sat four or five people away from me and called out from the other end of the table, "Hi Joe."

What...she noticed me! Holy crap! That cute girl from Mill Ave, who I hadn't stopped thinking about, by the way, just said hi. "Hey Nina, how are you?" I replied.

Instead of moving our seats and drawing attention to ourselves, we just talked back and forth from opposite ends of the table. The conversations around us faded into the background and it seemed like we were alone, just talking to get to know each other. My heart raced as we flirted back and forth. She'd give me a side smile and lean over to her sister, Noel, to say something, then back to the conversation. Occasionally, we'd be snapped back into the group conversation with an abrupt question about school, work, and the concert we'd just been to. After, Nina and I would slowly slide back into the silent background and talk. *Wow again*, I thought to myself. *Is this woman interested in me?* Oh, and of course everyone noticed us talking that night at Denny's, literally sitting between Nina and I, with front-row seats to see the beginning of the relationship. My hopes of meeting a woman who I enjoyed being around just became a reality. I guess the pastor from my previous church had been wrong. I wasn't out of God's will and it looked like He was about to bless me.

Since I hadn't seen Nina before the night at Mill Ave, I wasn't sure of the next time I would. She was flowing between two different groups, so her friends were never sure if she would be part of a hang-out, church event, or small group. To my pleasant surprise, she started hanging out with our small group more until it seemed as though I was seeing her all the time. Like most of the other people in the group, Nina was attending college. She was a vocal performance major at Phoenix College and she invited us to come to her concert. So, we all trekked down to the college to hear her sing. In a small rehearsal theater, Bret, our friend Candy, and I sat down in the squeaky, light blue seats and waited for the show to start. There wasn't a curtain, so when they were ready, the choir made their way to the stage and stood behind the piano.

Halfway through the performance, Nina walked over to stand next to the piano and began singing "In The Arms Of An Angel", by Sara McLauchlan. I was stunned. Her voice was warm, caring, and could pull you into the storyline of the music and lyrics. When she finished, we all clapped, and she walked back over to join the choir. After the concert, we all greeted and complimented her. "Nina, your voice is amazing! How did I not know this?" I said. She genuinely thanked me and greeted the rest of her friends. Soon, I found out Nina had been singing and performing since junior high. Part of the reason I didn't see her consistently was that she was singing on worship teams at a few other churches. I didn't think there was anything that could make Nina more attractive, but I was wrong. I could listen to her sing all day long. Her voice was so beautiful and it drew me in.

Over the next several months, I was intentional about seeing Nina as much as possible. If she was singing somewhere, I was there. Going to a coffee shop to hear someone play. Yep, let's go. Grabbing food after one of the many church services? Absolutely. I was obviously smitten. Anytime I was around her, it was as if we were the only ones in the room. We would talk for hours about life, family, church, and music. I had totally forgotten about Kara's warning, so in the summer of 2001, Nina and I began dating.

After a fourteen-hour trip to Northern California in her parents' minivan, with four other friends, we arrived at Mt Hermon. Everything seemed fine the entire trip. We held hands, called each other nicknames, and snuggled in the back seat when it was other people's turn to drive. After we unpacked the van and settled into the rooms – guys in one and ladies in another – Nina met me in the hallway, semi-smiled, and asked if we could talk. We went outside to the deck and sat down. There, she began to unpack her feelings and the struggle of still being in love with her ex-boyfriend.

"I'm really sorry, Joe. I didn't realize it until recently," she said through tears.

"Why did you wait until we got here? You know how awkward this is now? We still have three days together and then drive home. Seriously?! You're cruel." I got up and walked away.

I went back to my room to finish getting ready for dinner. I told the other two guys what happened. They didn't say much, their expressions were pretty clear though: "That sucks, bro." I barely spoke to Nina for the rest of the trip. I tried to enjoy myself, but most of the time I was irritated with anything Nina said or did. *Kara was right, damn it!* When we returned to Phoenix, the next few months were ugly. I was always rude and abrupt whenever I saw her, and she gave it back to me back in same measure.

I finally got over the breakup and moved on. It was difficult though, but Nina seemed to have cared about me. I had never really had someone give me that much attention. I still saw her at church, Tuesday night group, and whenever the group hung out. Her boyfriend was younger and part of a different crowd, so we didn't see him much. That relationship was short-lived though, I soon heard through the gossip chain that Nina broke up with him and was single again.

As the winter holidays approached, Nina and I started talking again. She was looking for a few people to sing with her for a Christmas caroling gig she had, and she asked me to join them. It gave us a chance to find some normalcy in our friendship. I really didn't have any interest in dating her again, given the previous breakup. She had trampled on my heart, my feelings were hurt, and I didn't think she was genuinely sorry about it. Maybe I had just been another guy showing her attention and she got caught up in all of it. So, I just didn't give her access to that part of myself. I had spent most of my life compartmentalizing things to keep safe, so this was just another one of those relationships. Even with all of that going on inside my head, she could still catch my attention so quickly, though. We could joke around, be witty, and talk about anything. She was still so beautiful Damn it!

By spring, Nina transferred to Grand Canyon University and was on a full ride scholarship for vocal performance. That brought a lot more concerts which I was happy to attend. I decided to move on, there wasn't a reason why we couldn't be friends, and, hey, we enjoyed being around each other, so why wouldn't we? The universe had different plans for us, though. The women of the group had a girls' night where Nina shared that she realized she had messed up with me the previous summer. The news made it to me pretty quickly. How did I feel about that? I internalized what it meant. *What if she breaks up with me again? Can I trust her? The first time, she hurt my feelings, the next time would break my heart. I don't know if I have the strength to endure that again in this life.* It took a few weeks before the topic came up between the two of us. We had finished a Thursday night church service and we all went back to our friend's house to watch Friends and Smallville. Nina asked if we could talk, so we went outside. She shared what I already knew and asked me how I felt. So, how did I feel? Scared, excited, and still completely smitten with her. I told her we would give it another chance.

I decided there was one last thing she needed to know before we could really move forward in our relationship. It was the worst part of me. The thing I hated; it was shameful, dirty. It lived in the desolate place in my mind. Apart from experimenting with my friend in high school and occasional bouts of porn, the beast had never been released from its confinement. It was forced to reside away from any part of my life, lest it bleed over, lest it be discovered. It was sitting there in isolation, constantly being scolded. I kept reinforcing; it was bad and there was no place for it in my life. Now I decided I would have to tell Nina about this beast. If we were going to be together, she had to know.

I had rehearsed what to say, had enough information to be honest, vulnerable, and clear that it wouldn't be a problem. I also got a way for Nina to back out if it was too much for her. The moment finally came one night after dinner. "Hey, let's talk for a few minutes," I said nervously as we sat down on the couch in my apartment. The room was filled with the weight of the last fifteen years. My head told me this was a bad idea, but my heart was the driver this time. "I need to tell you something about my life." I went on to explain how I was sexually abused as a child and struggled with what Christians call same-sex attraction. We also talked about what happened with the guy in high school and the pornography issue. I said to her, "There was no place for being gay, I didn't even think of myself as gay. This wasn't the life I wanted. I longed to have a wife, kids, to be a good Christian and to be happy. I had gone through therapy and learned how to live with the issue, fighting the temptation of the 'thorn in my flesh.'"

"Okay, so what does that mean for us? Are you gay?" she asked.

"No, I'm not. It just comes up occasionally. I wanted you to know about my past and that I sometimes struggle with it. But I have strong boundaries around it. Some of the guys know as well, so I have some accountability."

Nina nodded in agreement. "Well, thanks for telling me. Then, I don't think it's a problem, as long as you have people to talk to. Honestly, I thought you were going to tell me you had a kid or something. We can deal with it, it's your past and you're doing something about it."

At that moment, I knew she was the one for me. Nina knew about the saddest part of me and still loved me. Finally, someone important in my life chose me. She was committed to me.

When people started graduating college, the next phase of life began marriage. Some of the other couples were now getting engaged, and we were attending several weddings. In September of the same year, it was my turn to get married. I proposed to Nina in front of our friends and family at a park in Old Scottsdale. Nina had grown up going to this park, and we had spent plenty of time there, together, and we had a lot of special moments. Prior to the proposal, I had coordinated with friends to meet us in front of the library after dinner. The plan was that Nina, her parents, my mom, and I would go to dinner, then tell her we'd 'go for a walk' in the park afterward. Nina's dad, Joe, had ordered Chianti at dinner and I drank two glasses. Not being someone who drinks at all, I was pretty relaxed by the time we started walking. As we came around the bend toward a large open space the park used for performances, we saw a group of twenty people standing in the glow of the streetlights. You could hear a guitar playing and there was small candles on the ground. I suggested we walk over to see what was happening. As we got closer Nina recognized our friends. They opened into a big circle.

Bret continued playing the guitar in the background, as I declared my love to Nina. A bit nervous now, I asked her to marry me. She said, "Yes!" We kissed and the crowd roared with applause, fireworks exploded in the air, and doves flew into the sky. Okay, maybe there weren't any fireworks or doves. I had found my home; a safe place. Young Joey no longer had to sleep on a couch, bounce from house to house or rely on others to fill in an absent parents gap. I had my person now.

I actually met Nina's parents, Joe and Nancy Barto, before I met Nina, when we were all volunteering as leaders in the junior and high school groups at church. Nancy was polite, soft-spoken, and had a beautiful smile. Joe was a jokester from the get-go. He was gregarious, funny, intellectual, and a storyteller. We got to know one another on a personal level when I sat next to them at a leadership meeting, one afternoon.

During lunch, I found out they had been at the church for twenty years with their three daughters, and they decided to volunteer for junior high as a way to stay connected with them. I met their oldest daughter, Noel, a few weeks before I met Nina. Their youngest, Sally, was in high school, I just hadn't made the correlation yet.

Joe and I connected quickly. He was easy to talk with, whether the topic was business, the geopolitical landscape, tech, church, God, family or work. He had decades of experience under his belt, gave insightful advice, and laughed at his mistakes with a sense of humility. He created a space that was comfortable, safe, and open.

When Joe learned my last name, he said, "That sounds like a made-up name."

I responded, "Actually, it is." I began to share about my mom leaving me and the fact that I didn't know my dad.

When he asked why I wasn't more messed up, I said it was because of the church taking care of me in high school and my relationship with God. He complimented me on my resilience and tenacity to not continue the cycle that had plagued my family.

When I knew things were getting serious with Nina, I also shared my same-sex attraction issue with her parents. Knowing this could be the end of the relationship with all of them, I waited until I was sure I wanted to marry Nina. Surprisingly, Joe responded with love and grace. "We all have crosses to bear," he said, and thanked me for being honest. They had really committed to getting to know me and not judging my past. They felt more like parents than anyone before in my life. When Nina and I got engaged, I asked if I could call Nancy and Joe, Mom and Dad. They lovingly accepted the newly bestowed titles.

Dad and I continued to deepen our relationship by intentionally spending time together. I had a Grand Canyon-sized hole in my heart from not having a present dad. He started filling this by showing me care and encouragement, giving me advice, and hugging me. He said he was proud and ended every conversation with, "I love you Joe." I felt like God had given me this amazing gift, a bride, a dad, and even a mom to fill in the gaps that my biological mom didn't have the capacity to fill.

In 2003, Nina and I married in a ceremony with two hundred of our 'closest' friends and family. Joe and Nancy's childhood church had beautiful wooden beams with stained glass, allowing the light to shower through the scenes of Christ's birth to resurrection. Our pastor, Dan, officiated our wedding. He had been there as our relationship blossomed and knew my story, struggles, and resilience of becoming a healthy man as Nina and I began to write who the Makstons were together. At the end of the ceremony, he introduced us as "Joe & Nina Makston, the first of the Makston generation." I was already overjoyed to marry my beautiful bride, and then my friend honored us with a proclamation of new chapters in the Makston legacy! He saw what was unwritten, and it said: This is a new beginning, a new life, a family with many firsts ahead of them.

I was fully head over heels with my new bride. Yet, dating was totally different from living together in a five-hundred-and-one-square-foot apartment. There were a few new things I discovered quickly. I didn't realize Christmas music could be played year-round, it sounds a little different in the middle of summer, in Phoenix. Nina loved playing The Carpenters Christmas, no matter the time of year. She could annihilate you at any board game and not think twice about it. Breakfast and several cups of coffee, with cream, at a local eatery, were part of her love language. She talks in her sleep, mostly about being carried away by balloons, riding around on roller skates, and picking things up. It took some getting used to.

Church was our main source of friendships and community. I served in the youth ministry and young adults' group. Nina sang in the worship and worked a few hours during the week on campus. Although we served in different ways, Nina and I had the same heart for people. We wanted them to feel connected and be part of a community that supported them. That same mindset was built into most of what we did, even down to where we lived our first year of marriage. Daniel, my best man, and his wife, Done, had rented an apartment in the same complex we were living in. We had a lot of dinners, game nights, movie fests, and time spent just sitting around talking. That spurred our desire to start a young married small group to gather the rest of our friends and talk about what it was like during the early years of marriage and having babies.

A week before our first anniversary, we found out we were pregnant. It was exciting and scary all at once. Nina still had another year of school and we were barely making ends meet as I had brought a significant amount of debt into the marriage. Preparing for a baby on top of our existing challenges as well was overwhelming. When we shared the news with Mom and Dad, they were also excited and a little nervous, as they recalled their first years with a baby. They had plenty of room in their house and told us we could move in with them. They brought us in so Mom would take care of the baby while Nina finished school, and we could use the money that would no longer be going to rent and utilities to pay down my debt. They helped us out multiple times and did it with such grace and generosity.

Living with Mom and Dad was quite enjoyable. They had a room on the first floor and with a baby coming, we took up two rooms on the second. Again, there were things that I had to get used to that I hadn't noticed when Nina and I were dating. Dad was an early riser. And he was loud! On mornings he wasn't traveling, he'd wake up to cook breakfast and sing while doing it. Pans and cupboards would bang and slam as he moved through the kitchen, while some sort of music would be playing on the Bose near the dining room table. The first time it happened, I laid in bed with Nina and asked, "What in the world is he doing down there?"

Half awake, she laughed and said, "Making breakfast. You'll get used to it."

And I did. I also had to get used to loading the dishwasher – there's a right and wrong way to do it. Frozen berries, apples, baby spinach, and pretzels were staples in the house. Lastly, Dad loved celebrating anything that gave him an excuse to grill steaks or order food in. I enjoyed this part of life since I hadn't experienced it very much growing up. I had a pretty plain palate, so being exposed to Lebanese, Chinese, and Greek food was an adventure. The pinnacle was going for sushi though. A lot of Dad's work was in Asia, so he knew the best places in Phoenix to get great sushi. It was the norm for the Barto family to eat like this, but I hadn't experienced the beauty of food like this before. I would say it's one of Dad's love languages and I certainly felt loved.

We settled into the new pace of life in the Bartos' house in just enough time to begin preparing for our son to be born. One of the great things about being in a church community is that there are a lot of other young families. Several of our friends from the young married small group had kids outgrowing clothes, cribs, and car seats, so they passed them along to us. We had a few baby showers later and we were ready for the little man to arrive. There was just one question left: *How the hell do we do this?*

Second Gen

As Nina's due date came and passed, she got more uncomfortable and restless, while I got more excited and anxious about what was about to happen. I had been on the merry-go-round of thoughts of whether I could actually be a good dad. I'd wonder, *What if I screw this kid up and he turns out like me? I don't even know how to be a dad.* Yet, there wasn't a lot I could do. He was still coming and I needed to figure out how to get over that insecurity.

Our small group had two mentor couples who were further along on their parenting journey and were there for just this type of issue. One of the men, Kent, had had a childhood similar to mine and he was able to overcome it. He always greeted me with a tight hug and a hard slap on the back, then looked me in the eyes to ask how I was doing. He was intentional, fully present, caring, and loved spending time with his wife and kids. He was genuine in how he felt, willing to share both the story of his past and what he was doing now to stay engaged in his marriage and fatherhood. I felt like I could ask Kent anything and he could relate. I shared my worries about not feeling like I would be a good dad to him and he helped me believe that it was possible; I'd just have to put the work in. Things didn't change overnight, but at the very least, there was someone that I could talk with about it, which was comforting. Now, I was flanked by Kent and Dad to help along the way.

The next generation of Makston came into our lives in February of 2005. Eli Joseph was born that evening with a few whimpers and a fist in his mouth. With cone-shaped noggin, they cleaned him off and handed him to me. With all the joy and pride a first-time dad owns, through happy tears, I greeted my little man.

Eli was easy going right off the bat – well, once we figured out that he was constantly hungry and started giving him formula. Mornings were a special time for the two of us, which helped Nina since she wasn't an early riser. Often, he'd be awake before me, and just lay in his crib until I got him to make our way downstairs for a bottle. Mom or Dad would usually be there to greet us, then I'd sit at the table with Eli in my lap and read the newspaper out loud to him.

During his first year, he continually had a furrowed brow. He'd have this serious look in his eye, then squish up his eyebrows. Our friends would ask if he was mad about something. It took us quite some time to realize he wasn't mad, but trying to process what he was seeing. He didn't like his hands dirty, and if they were, he would walk around with fists until we could wipe them off. He could put a small puzzle together in a few minutes, play by himself for hours, and preferred to build Legos on his own so he could figure out the mechanics. Even as a baby, his brain was always working to understand how something worked.

Eli has a deep compassion for people, asks questions to understand, and support you even if he doesn't agree. Just don't be a jerk; he has a low tolerance for people who are unkind. He is the gatherer in his friend group and works to help people feel included. He is the spitting image of me, for better or worse. Whenever I'd meet a teacher or parent, as soon as I'd walk in, they'd say, "Oh you're Eli's dad. He looks just like you." Eli you're welcome!

Ava Nicole, whom we call Mars, joined the Makstons in March of 2007. She came into the world literally with her mouth wide open. When she was born and the nurse brought her to the bassinet to clean her off, she was screaming. The only thing I could think to say was, "Her mouth is so big, Nina." That mouth was ready to challenge the world's thinking right away and continues to bring new perspectives into our home, most of the time with such grace. When Mars was a baby, she shared a room with Eli. Early in the morning, I'd hear Eli talking to her, showing different stuffed animals through the slats of her crib and showing her books. By the time we'd go in to get them up for the day, Mars' crib would be full of animals and books.

Mars' curiosity was all about being creative and testing the limits. She loved climbing trees, along with falling and jumping out of them. That caused multiple trips to the ER. She found ways to express herself through drawing, making animals out of Play-Doh, painting, and dressing herself. That typically meant mismatched clothes, galoshes, and one of my hats. Mars had a great sense of humor too, always trying to get people to laugh by being silly or crossing her eyes. She would practice doing it in the back seat of the car. "Hey, dad. Look!" she'd call out. She'd smile, then cross one eye, then the other. We'd crack up and she'd go back to playing.

From a young age, Mars marched to her own beat; it's one of her gifts. She's regularly felt comfortable with who she is and will not conform to the norms of society. Early on, she would pull hair ties out of her hair. I'd look in the rearview mirror and see her head shaking as she yanked the little bands out of her ponytails so she could play with her hair. As she got older, her friend group consisted of kids that didn't fit into the standard kid model of boys playing sports and girls playing with dolls. If someone was different, she wanted to get to know them. Similar to Eli, she had the capacity to show high levels of compassion and inclusion. It's amazing what kids are able to do just naturally.

The first few years of being a dad were rough. Not because of the kids, but because I truly thought there was no way I could be a good dad. I had somehow convinced myself that I would ruin them and they wouldn't want to spend time with me. Even though I believed that lie, my kids did not. I was their hero. As soon as I would get home from work, they would immediately be ready to play and talk about their day. Nina would be exhausted and in need of a break, so it was a perfect time for me to get down on the floor and play cars, Legos, or watch the performance they had been practicing all afternoon. Weekends were full of bike rides, costume parties, the park, and building forts with couch cushions and blankets – just like I did with my brother when I was a kid. By the time I had several Father's Days under my belt, I had begun experiencing a shift in my thinking. I'd always wanted to be a good dad, fully present and encouraging to my kids, and I think I was actually moving in that direction. It took a long time to stop believing the lies. Luckily, Eli and Mars continue to reinforce that I am a good dad through their words and actions.

Even through my insecurity, I truly loved every season of being a dad. I had gotten a lot of practice with my sisters' kids when I was in high school, and now I could use that with my own kids. When they were babies, middle-of-the-night feedings were moments I could talk with them and pray for the life I hoped for. If Nina was singing at the church on the weekend, I'd have one of the kids strapped to me in a sling and the other would be in childcare. As they got older, I took them to the library on the weekend to check out stacks of books. From the moment we got in the car, they'd each pull out a book and flip through them cover to cover, then grab the next one. By the time we got home, books would be all over the back seat and the bag empty and Eli and Mars would be holding whatever book they wanted me to read first when we get inside. When they went to elementary school, I'd pick up their favorite lunch and show up at school to eat with them. They'd have no idea I was coming and the sheer joy and surprise on their faces when they walked out of class to see me standing there with lunch was always magical. There were Cub Scouts and one season of soccer with Eli – he truly is my son and doesn't love sports – and countless musical performances with Mars. Those moments gave me a chance to learn I didn't need to fit into a dad mold. I had spent so much time worried about it that I didn't realize I was being the dad that Eli and Mars needed. We were an unconventional family and didn't need to do or be like the rest of the families at church or school. That was a relief for me and Nina. She was never a 'mommy, mom' who loved pink bows and fancy dresses. She was practical and functional, which was a good fit for our family.

A few months before Mars was born, our family hit a busy Christmas season. I was a staff pastor and Nina was on the worship team. We'd minister at the four services, then go to her parents' house for the Barto family Christmas party, where everyone from Joe's side of the family would join in the celebration.

My mom, Kathy, was visiting and planned to attend the last service, then join us for the Bartos' party. Normally, she didn't like to be with anyone on Christmas. She preferred to visit a couple of weekends before, have a small Christmas dinner, and then open presents. When she said she wanted to be with us for the holiday, it was a big deal and one of the few times our families would be together.

It had already been a long day of preparations and getting Eli in and out of daycare. Between services, I carried him in a sling and said goodbye to one group of people as the new group arrived. Twenty minutes before the last service started, I was expecting Mom to come in, but instead, my brother, Pat, called.

He immediately cut to the chase, "Hey man, what did you do to Mom?"

Not knowing what he was talking about, I said, "Nothing." To the best of my knowledge, she was on her way to meet us at the church. He had other intel though; She was on her way home and not going to the party. I didn't believe him because we had talked a few hours before.

Pat replied, "No joke, man. Whatever you did pissed her off and she's on her way home right now."

I hung up to call Mom and got her voice mail. "Hey Mom, just checking to see if you're on your way to church. We're starting soon. Give me a call." She didn't show up for the service, so I texted her. No response. I called her after the service, no answer. I sent another text and still nothing. I started to get worried and checked in with my siblings. They all heard from her that Christmas Eve and the following Christmas Day. Four days later, she finally texted me that she was okay.

As Nina and I processed the events of the past few days, I was reminded of how terrible my family had been at communicating when I was growing up. If someone got mad, they would just blow up, yell at you, then stew about it for weeks, or ignore you completely, in some cases for months. We were exposed to all levels of trauma growing up – drugs, alcohol, sex, domestic violence, guns – because we had no boundaries. People didn't really talk about boundaries in the 80s and 90s. It was a little too 'hippy-dippy'. I had recently read a book called *Boundaries,* by Henry Cloud and John Townsend, which had really motivated me to think about the subject in a different way. I now realized that none of my relationships ever really had emotional boundaries, because I had been living in a constant state of abandonment and neglect. Setting an emotional and physical boundary with Mom would be new for me and I needed to be clear about expectations.

It was a Tuesday night and I was an hour away from starting a college group ministry when my phone rang. I paused for a moment, wondering if I really had the time and emotional capacity to talk to my mom. "Hey, Mom," I finally answered. She was brief, and said she wanted to let me know she was okay. I asked her what had happened, why she had left and hadn't returned my calls or texts. She explained that she didn't think it was fair that she had to share a holiday with the Bartos; she should be able to spend the entire time with just us. It became clear that this was a power play for Mom to get what she wanted. When she didn't, she took her emotional ball and went home.

I told her, "Mom, I get it and I think it's okay that you want to have the holiday with us, but you need to tell us. We can't read your mind." I went on to explain that this was a new stage of life for me and for our relationship. "We have to figure out a way to navigate this, if we don't talk about it now, we're going to have this conversation again. There are some things I know and there are some things I don't know. What I know is that we want you in our lives; it's important for you to have a relationship with the kids, with me, with Nina. I also know that this isn't the way Makstons deal with conflict. If we just shut down, it doesn't do anybody any good. We need to be in a space where we can talk. It may not be right away, and I think that is absolutely fine. One of us may have to say, 'Hey, I'm having a hard time with this right now, but I'm not ready to talk about it.' That's what I expect in my relationships with you, with my friends, with my family, even at work. If you want to be able to spend time with us, I need you to be able to show up that way. It doesn't have to be pretty. We're all learning to have good boundaries. But if you just shut down, decide not to talk to us, and go home, I have to draw a hard line. I want to spend time with you, which means we have to build a healthy relationship and learn how to communicate well with each other. How do you feel about that?"

With her one-word response of "Okay," a new level of communication and healthier boundaries were set in motion. It didn't happen overnight, we had to lay a lot of groundwork, but it started a new story for us. Later, I thought that maybe this was the first time someone approached her about setting healthy boundaries and gave her space to talk. Maybe she was learning too. It was a slow and sometimes frustrating process, but we began to set new norms with her.

I was the last child in my family to have kids. My siblings experienced Mom as a grandma who was very similar to the Mom we'd grown up with. There was a lot of yelling and demanding that they do things for her, treating her grandchildren the way she treated us growing up – even Mom disciplining them, which never went well. My sisters had to draw a hard line after Mom became physically violent with their kids on two separate occasions. I knew about this and was worried about exposing my children to it. Even though we were working on new boundaries and a different way of living, Mom could go off the rails at any time. We would have to take things very slowly, and I didn't feel comfortable leaving her alone with the kids.

Her first visit after the boundary conversation felt different. She brought coloring books and crayons and sat down to color with the kids. I had never seen Mom do this with my nieces or nephews. Next, she played some board games and finally went outside to play soccer. I thought, *"Who is this woman? I have never seen Mom run in my entire life. Now she is running around, kicking a ball with my kids, reading books, and playing with them."* There was pure joy on her face. She was having the time of her life. I know my siblings had had conversations with Mom about how she acted with their families and it never really changed, so I was surprised to see a different side of her. She didn't raise her voice on me. If she talked down on the kids, I would certainly say something. She really wanted to spend time with us. I'd like to think this was because we approached the conversation differently to show her honor and respect.

Boundaries can be tricky when we're not aware of them. It can feel like we are behind a concrete wall with watchtowers and barbed wire, in a valley of open land where people can roam freely, or a white picket fence with a clearly defined gate. It's all about our history, how self-aware we are, and whether we've done the work to heal from it. When Mom left that Christmas, we had to choose to create a new path for our relationship. I had to build the fence and lead her to the gate, so I could give her access to our family. This experience taught me that it's okay to let people know what you need and when they might be invading your personal space.

New Dad

Living with Joe and Nancy when Eli was born helped us out, both financially and with childcare. I had bought a brand-new car six months before we got married, on top of my already existing several thousands of dollars in credit card debt. Needless to say, I wasn't very good with money and growing up didn't have anyone to show me how to manage a budget or what it meant to save. I had no idea what 'being good' with money looked like.

Nina and I had been surviving on a single-family income since we got married. Even after paying off all the credit card debt, things were still tight, and it was difficult for me to talk about money. I was embarrassed that I didn't know how to manage it very well and so, I didn't include her in paying the bills.

Now, I had messed up balancing the checkbook and overdrawn the account. Knowing we needed to buy groceries and pay a few bills; I couldn't keep it from her. This wasn't the first time, but it was still humbling to tell my wife I had messed up. Her parents had always been supportive of us having a good foundation, so I suggested asking them for help. Nina said, "Yeah, I'm sure they would help. Why don't you call Dad?"

We'd only make it another week before we were in serious trouble, so I needed to connect with Dad pretty quickly. Later that morning, I picked up the phone to call him. "Hey, Dad, I messed up on our finances and overdrew our account. Can you and Mom help us out?" I paused anxiously, waiting to be lectured for 'not being good'. "Yeah, Son, let's see how we can help. How about we meet up for lunch," he suggested. I shouldn't have been shocked, but I was. Dad and Mom had already helped us so much and he was willing to do it again.

The following day, Dad and I sat down at a BBQ joint close to my office, where we caught up on life, work, the kids, and Nina.

"So, Joe, tell me what happened," he finally asked.

I explained, "I hadn't accounted for a bill and had overdrawn the account. It wasn't like we were spending money on things we couldn't afford, I had learned that lesson. I had just made a mistake."

"You know, I couldn't manage a checkbook when we were first married either. We barely made ends meet." He shared his own experience of being in a similar position. Dad and I talked through how much I needed, and he handed me a check. He didn't scold or ask me to pay him back, he just gave me a check.

"Thanks, Dad. That is really kind of you and Mom to help us out," I humbly said.

"Of course, you're our son. We love you and Nina. These are tough lessons to learn, and we're glad we can help." We hugged and parted ways.

Dad has this keen ability to savor life. He's never in too much of a hurry to get to the next thing. He'd rather sit down at a restaurant and tell stories as we ate. I rarely lived in the moment, so it was difficult to settle and just enjoy what was happening right now. This is when Dad introduced me to cognac and cigars. I had never really drunk or smoked a cigar worth remembering, but he told me I just hadn't smoked a good one. He bought my first bottle of cognac after a big job interview that seemed like an easy win, though I didn't get the job. He said, "Well, it was either going to be to congratulate you or commiserate together. I guess it's the latter. Sorry, son." This turned into a monthly event where they would come over for dinner. Mom and Nina would put the kids to bed while Dad and I would head out to the backyard. We'd light up a cigar as Dad spoke about where they were made and taught me how to puff on it. I'd pour us a drink, then we'd sit and talk for hours. We called this 'solving the world's problems.' It was just time for a dad and his son to check in on work, the marriage, kids, and church, and for him to share what new business ventures he was about to take on.

When I was searching for my dad in my twenties and aimlessly trying to answer the big questions of life, I had imagined having a dad like Joe. Someone who just wanted to spend time with his son, talk about life, share his wisdom, and could chat with me about most any topic. Beyond that, though, it's the way he goes about it that matters. He does it with such intention and sincerity. Dad is okay asking difficult questions and sharing how he feels about them. His hugs are full of sincerity, warmth, and comfort, as if his entire body and soul collectively say, "I love you, Son. You are so important to me. I'm proud of who you are," all at once. Now, we'll probably never backpack along the Oregon coast, ride bikes through Bryce Canyon, or hike

Kilimanjaro. I'm totally fine with that. I'd rather call him on the phone to say, "Hi Dad, I miss you," and hear him respond, "I miss you too, Son. I love you." He never told me to be good. Instead, he made me feel that I belonged.

The Good Life

We continued to figure out what life was like for the Makstons. We were okay with not scheduling every moment of our evenings and weekends with kids' activities. We tried sports for a short season but the kids hated it. Hiking worked well until they could walk and say how much hiking sucked. So, that wasn't our thing, that's okay, we just had to figure out what was. That's where music came in.

Nina grew up with great music from Harry Connick Jr, Frank Sinatra, Fleetwood Mac, The Carpenters, and maybe too much Family Life Radio. Music was just a part of us. I wasn't as skilled, nor did I have the memory to remember every word of a song like Nina and the kids, but it was our thing. Eli and Mars took to music very early, and the car became the space where we could belt it out as a family. I did contribute show tunes to the family though. It must have been all those Kids Incorporated, Mickey Mouse Club, church musicals, and 90s Disney cartoons I loved so much. Either way, music is part of who we were Makstons.

Although I don't enjoy singing Christmas music in the middle of summer, I do enjoy singing it during the actual holidays. Even before the kids were born, Nina and I would drive around listening to Christmas music and looking for Christmas lights. Whenever we found a house with way too many of them, we'd drive by and scream "MERRY CHRISTMAS" at the top of our lungs. We scared the kids the first few times we did it with them, but they caught on pretty quickly and couldn't wait to do it again. Yes, we have found our groove as a family. Some amazing traditions were created as well, like homemade cards for special events, 'dad dates,' forts, movie nights on a pile of blankets and pillows and game nights.

Hollywood tells us when things are going smoothly, that's usually when a plot twist is thrown in, the dramatic music queues up. Nina and I served in separate areas of the church on the weekends. This required her to be at worship team practice during the week. I was leading a men's group on another night, and then we were both training for races on our own. As the holidays approached, Nina was spending long hours at church in the evenings, while I was home with the kids. On top of that, she was singing in a caroling group, which meant more rehearsals and performances. To say we were busy was an understatement. Still, I thought we just needed to get through the holidays, we had done this before and used to the pressures of little time together. When the holidays were over, things would slow down and we could focus on family again.

As the New Year came and went, our schedules did slow down, but Nina seemed to be off. She was still spending a lot of time at church late into the evening and going out with friends afterwards.

When I came home from work one night, the house was quiet.

"Where are the kids?" I asked.

"They're with friends. I think we need to talk."

Like years ago, when I had sat nervously on my couch to tell her about being attracted to guys, this was not going to be a pleasant conversation. But now, I was the recipient of bad news. As I slowly put my things away and sat down, she began to cry. Over the next hour, the last seven years of our marriage unraveled. Nina had crossed a line with several guys on the worship team. One guy found out about another and threatened to tell the pastor. To prevent that, she wanted to tell me and she said it wouldn't happen again. My heart sank into my stomach, all my muscles tensed up, tears welled up in my eyes, but I wouldn't let them fall down my face. As I sat there listening to her explain how it all started, I began to ask myself, *What the hell is going on? This wasn't the plan. We're supposed to be better than this! I placed my trust in this women, is she just like Mom?*

Maybe I should have been more upset, yelled at her, even asked her to leave. But I loved Nina. She was a wonderful mom and she was 'my person.' I shifted to wondering what I had done wrong to make her share this part of herself with someone else. I had kept the beast that lived in the desolate place in check. When it did stir, I shared it with my guy friends to help me through it – Nina interrupted my train of thought, "It's not your fault, Joe. You're a great husband and dad. I'm just fucked up. I'm sorry, I need help."

We had developed deep relationships at New Hope. It was where Nina had grown up, become a worship leader, and I had been a staff pastor. Now, it was a place of pain, sorrow, and broken trust from Nina and those men. Nina's devastating news brought clarity that this was no longer a healthy place for our family, and we made the equally devastating decision to leave.

Nina was already planning a trip out of town that same week, so I told her she still had to go to give me time to process what had happened. When Nina left for her trip, Dad and Mom reached out to come over. After dinner, Mom put the kids to bed while Dad and I went outside. The first thing he said when he sat down was, "I'm sorry my daughter did this to you, Joe. Whatever happens with you two, you're still our son and we want to be a part of your life." He gave me a hug as I cried, trying to understand what I had done wrong for my wife to do this. Mom joined us a few minutes later and said the same thing. They told me I still belonged and part of their family. Yet, it didn't completely quiet my fears. I was not only worried about losing my marriage but everything that had come with it.

Nina's willingness to see a relationship therapist to understand what went wrong and why, gave me hope that this had been an isolated incident. Maybe we could recover from this. However, we didn't see much improvement in our relationship or in Nina's understanding of why until she started seeing her own therapist. She had to start unpacking unresolved issues from her childhood. Similarly, I was still working through my own mom issues and realizing I had allowed Nina to fill the void left behind. We now had a decision to make. Were we willing to put our marriage first, even before the kids? It took years to rebuild trust and we wanted to take the time to heal together. We both had shit to work through, so we continued with therapy. It was painful and we struggled to create new boundaries, but it was worth it. We learned a lot about ourselves, the wounds that still needed to heal, how to emotionally show up better, and our love for each other and our family. All of this led us to a new church, friends, and better boundaries. When the time was right, we even shared our experiences with other couples to encourage them to make their marriage a priority.

After leaving New Hope, we were looking for a new place to call home. Some people told us about a Saturday church service, full of young families, down the street. As we walked through the front doors, someone called from behind, "Nina Barto! Is that you?" This was a regular occurrence for us. We'd often run into one of her high school friends, a teacher, or a parent from one of the many activities she was involved in. She turned around, said hello, and introduced me. It was a little comforting that we knew someone. Maybe this would be the place we'd call home.

All my life, I have wanted to be accepted and feel like I belonged. As I tried to figure myself out and understand the kind of people I wanted to be close to, a common theme of meaningful conversations about what was really going on kept coming to the surface. Yes, the high-level stuff is valuable. It creates relatability. Tell me about your day, how your vacation was, what restaurant you eat at, I want to hear about that. But I also want to know the things you think no one cares about, or maybe you're too scared, ashamed, or afraid to say out loud. I can't be your therapist, but I want to hear about that part of your life. When I was at New Hope, I had developed these kinds of friendships with some of the guys. They knew about all the good things that were happening, some of my childhood, and even that I was attracted to men. I didn't want to hide any part of myself, and I needed a safe space to alleviate the shame I continued to feel about something I couldn't get rid of. These few men were kind and supportive. The goal was to continue living a full life as a straight man, married to a woman, and raising a family. It took more than my strength to do that. When the beast tried to stir, I could count on these guys. In a short time, the feeling would subside and I'd be back to 'normal.'

Matt was my first church friend. I was still trying to heal and didn't want to make an effort to meet anyone. However, Nina and Matt's fiancǔe, Lindsey, met in a women's Bible study and decided we should get to know each other. They awkwardly introduced us after church one weekend and mentioned that Matt led the men's study group. *"Ah, I see what you're doing here, ladies. Trying to appeal to my desire to have a meaningful relationship with men. Damn, you got me,"* I thought. Although I wasn't keen on it, Matt seemed like a great guy and was passionate about men encouraging each other, so I asked if I could join his group. That was the beginning of an amazing friendship, both in and out of church.

As I got to know Matt, I learned that he was a brilliant entrepreneur, which usually meant he had multiple irons in the fire and could talk endlessly about margins and returns. He was a country boy who loved the woods and squirrel hunting, and he had a deep love for Jesus. He was raised in the church and had recently rededicated his life as an adult. He didn't want to wait for someone else to tell him how to do anything, so he started his own Bible study. Matt and I spent a lot of time together in those first few months, especially since I didn't know many other people. But the church began to grow, and so did the group that Matt was leading, so we decided to move it to my house. This was the beginning of several groups starting and continuing to grow, all because of his heart to help men talk about the Bible.

When Matt and I moved the group to my house, I wanted the guys to feel comfortable just walking in, no need to ring the doorbell. Everybody had the right to use the fridge and make themselves comfortable. They could sit wherever they wanted, even in the corner of the couch – which was usually my spot. After thirty minutes of catching up, eating snacks, and decompressing from the day, we'd settle into my living room to get to know each other better. If we had anyone who could play guitar, we'd sing a few songs. Then, I'd usually lead the discussion from the Bible or a study guide we'd picked up along the way. While reading Scripture was important, I wanted to focus more on building relationships and having a consistent group of men to walk with in life.

The normal 'bro code' buffer of one guy per couch disappeared as we became more comfortable with each other. Then, more people started to show up. A whole new level of comfort was required, and we all had to get over the awkwardness of our hairy legs touching to squeeze another guy on the couch. When it became clear that this wasn't going to work, we gathered chairs from the rest of the house to form a second row behind the couch. There was so much energy in the room that people began to share how they felt about the scriptures, what was happening at home, work, and in their hearts. Our small group quickly became large and outgrew my living room. My closest friends came from leading a small group with Matt. Even after he moved on to other things, we stayed connected and he'd join us when he could.

Another friend I met in church was Aaron, who I noticed early on along with his wife in our Saturday night services. His presence was a little intimidating to me, so I didn't interact with him much. He had a bit of a stern face, was fit, and carried himself like he was one of the cool kids. I never fit into that category, so I purposely kept my distance. I quickly realized I was making wild assumptions when we were finally introduced by our pastor at a church movie night. Aaron and Becca sat behind my family as we watched Charlie Brown Christmas, and were appalled at the way those kids talked to each other. Our pastor came over to say hello and asked if Aaron and I had met. I hadn't realized they were sitting behind us and now I was in a full-blown meet and greet.

I soon learned that Aaron loved to hike, was a hard worker, ran a tortoise farm out of his backyard, and was always looking to start a new business. I said to myself, "*Wait a minute, this guy is pretty cool. I'm so stupid for being intimidated.*" We started hanging out a little bit more as our families got to know each other. Aaron was a bit of a smart-ass to begin with, which I came to appreciate about him. I was a pretty serious guy most of the time, so when he'd have a quick joke in a text thread or with the guys, I'd laugh so hard. I liked seeing that part of him.

Aaron and Becca had just bought a house nearby, and soon after we met needed help moving. Sunday afternoon, I got a text from Aaron, "Hey, we're moving on Thursday and need some help. Are you available?"

"*Who the hell moves on a Thursday?* I thought to myself." "Yeah, sure. I can help after work. Probably around 5:30 or 6. Is that okay?"

"Sure, just text me and I'll let you know where we are."

That Thursday, I finished work, changed in my car, and drove over to his house. When I arrived, Matt was already there, loading the trailer that Aaron had borrowed. We greeted each other, hugged, and I asked how I could help.

"Well, we're in the back of the house. I have some bricks for the tortoise in the backyard that should be the last thing to load." Matt looked at me with a small grin.

Aaron had mentioned that he had a turtle 'hobby,' but this was no hobby. It was a full-fledged habitat, with sections to separate different species, and it took up most of the backyard. I had expected ten or fifteen stones, but we loaded and unloaded hundreds.

Over the next few weeks, I helped Aaron and Becca settle into their new home. A friendship was formed as we worked side by side, going through each room, painting, hanging ceiling fans, rearranging furniture, and moving bricks for the tortoises several times.

Since Aaron enjoyed hiking so much, I asked him to join me on a Friday morning. Being together in a small group was good for us and our community, but Aaron preferred one-on-one time, outside, doing physical activities. I was totally on board, and it turned into almost ten years of spending Friday mornings together.

I looked forward to those mornings; getting up before sunrise, then driving to the trailhead parking lot to wait for Aaron. We'd hug and start the hike up, whatever mountain we'd decided to tackle. The initial pleasantries would be exchanged as we walked to the trailhead. "So how was your week?" "Good" "Busy" "Tiring," would be the regular responses.

When you know you're going to be with someone for an extended period of time, you have to make a decision quickly. Are we going to stay on a high level or go deep? It doesn't have to be one or the other, but if you stay at a high level for too long, in my experience, it's difficult to transition to going deeper. I am an out-loud processor, whereas Aaron is the opposite. I could go deep quickly to get things off the table that I had been working through in my head. Because Aaron was different, I learned to ask him more questions in the beginning so that he felt comfortable sharing what he needed. It ended up being a good cadence for both of us. Our hikes became a place where we could talk freely about almost anything. We'd challenge each other on our relationship with God, church, struggles, family, and work. We'd ask each other questions, share advice, and process how we felt about a variety of topics or issues. Aaron and I had busy lives with growing families, work, and church commitments, so we didn't get much time together outside of Friday mornings. That's why this time became sacred and really housed ninety percent of our friendship. We would move mountains to make sure we could get together once a week if Friday didn't work with our schedules.

It was through these friendships that I learned the value of being as authentic as possible. I made the decision to share my own struggles when the time was right and in the moments that mattered. At first, I didn't think anyone wanted to hear about the difficult parts of life. But the reality was that they did, and maybe for the first time, they could also breathe a sigh of relief that they were not alone. Surprisingly, guys would often say, "I needed to hear that. Thank you for sharing the hard parts of your life. I thought I was the only one who felt that way." I couldn't put it into words then, but I wanted to be part of a community of men where we could share the deepest parts of ourselves, celebrate each other, go on adventures, and grow together. We didn't have to go through life alone. There was a place where you could hear someone other than your wife and kids say you're pretty cool and you bring value to this earth. And I was going to need that sooner than expected.

Shots

Nina had doubled down on getting in shape, so she hiked and ran on a regular basis. Trail running became my new best friend and a way for me to connect with God. We had gotten to a fitness level where we thought it would be fun to run a race together. Yes, we were 'those' people. 5 AM had always been way too early for Nina, but now, she was up and at 'em. When it was still dark outside and quite chilly, we headed north thirty minutes to Cave Creek. When we reached the trailhead, there was a sea of runners, in their short shorts, all huddled together trying to keep warm. Just before the sun peeked over the mountain, we took a deep breath as the countdown started. The whistle blew and we all started running over the timer belt that initiated our trackers. The 5K would take us up and down a loop of narrow trails, lined with blooming cacti. After Nina and I separately crossed the finish line, we congratulated each other. We collected our participation metals, then headed home to shower and rest before we had to pick up the kids from Mom and Dad's house. We turned in early that evening, still recovering from the adrenaline crash and having been ill-prepared for the steep hills we climbed earlier that day.

The next morning was Easter Sunday and the sun broke just a little brighter through the night sky. The kids opened their baskets, we went to church, and then we were off to a traditional Easter picnic with Nina's extended family. After the egg hunt, a few rounds of the putting green, eating lunch, and a slice of lamb cake – *yes, I did say lamb cake, Google it, it's a thing* – it was time to relax on a blanket under the trees. My left eye had been bothering me since I'd woken up that morning. I had suffered from migraines since I was a kid and assumed it was probably one coming on. Maybe I was just tired from the race or something was up with my contact. The next morning as I was getting ready for work, I put in my contacts and realized I couldn't see out of my left eye. I thought maybe I had torn my lens so I put a new one in, that didn't fix it. Now I was getting worried. As soon as my eye doctor opened, I called and they asked me to come in immediately. After ruling out a blood clot and aneurysm, I was referred to a neurologist.

Over the next few months, we lived in uncertainty about what was really happening. The doctors thought it was Lupus, Lyme disease, or maybe Multiple Sclerosis. Between MRIs of my brain and spinal taps, it took six months to confirm what it was. My eyesight had begun to improve, but I was exhausted all the time, I couldn't concentrate, and struggled to put words together. In October of 2010, Nina and I sat down in my neurologist's office, where he began to lay out what they had discovered. "You have Multiple Sclerosis, Joe. The good thing is, we caught it early and it's treatable," the doctor explained.

As his words penetrated my ears, they pushed me outside of my body into the room, to watch everything unfold as an observer. My hearing was muffled and my vision became blurry like the beginning of a dream sequence.

The doctor's voice brought me back to consciousness. "What questions do you have?"

I blinked and looked up, "Um, medication? You said I can take medication?" He nodded and walked through the process of giving myself daily shots, then he handed Nina a brochure on this specific medication. He shook our hands and said this really was the best news we could get. Then, he sent us home to take time to process everything.

Two weeks later, a nurse came to our home and showed me how to administer my daily shot. I would need to rotate each day through six different places in my upper thigh, stomach, and my triceps. I could never reach the back of my arm, so Nina needed to help me for the first several months. After being diagnosed, we decided to tell the kids that I had to give myself shots, so I could stay healthy. We didn't want to scare them, so we had them join us when the nurse was there. That helped a ton, as they could see what the shot did and the nurse could answer questions. Eli and Mars were five and three, and they were more curious to see than asking questions. MS had to be part of who we were as a family now. We chose not to let it consume us, but those first few years were emotionally taxing for all of us.

What's more, Nina and I hadn't yet fully healed from what happened at New Hope. I was still struggling with trusting her. Now I had to depend on her as I adapted to the medication, and she took on more responsibility with the kids when I was having an episode. It was agonizing to have to ask for help from someone that didn't trust. Even with all the work we had done through therapy, I still had a thought in the back of my head, *Does she really want to be here? Is she actually being honest now?* There wasn't a way of knowing, and if we were going to make it, I needed to depend on her more now than ever before.

I had to now learn the two sides to MS; the physical limitations, like the issue with my eye, and also the emotional toll it would take on us. At first, I didn't want Nina and the kids to worry more than they already had over the past six months. I had felt pretty hopeless though. Being exhausted all the time, struggling to put my words together, and my eye continuing to lose sight, then come back suddenly – it was too much for me on my own. Thankfully, a friend of mine knew someone who had been diagnosed several years earlier and connected us. The best advice he shared was to talk about what people cannot see.

"Your emotions and mind will be challenged constantly. Most of MS is unseen by the world around you. That means you have to let the people that matter into that part of your life. You're going to have to share when you're depressed, when your legs feel so heavy that you can barely get out of bed, and even why you're so angry because you can't say the words that your brain is trying to get out of your mouth. That's part of your responsibility to Nina and your kids. Your family has to live with MS, not just you."

Those were difficult words to hear from someone I didn't know very well, but he was right. I couldn't hold back what I was experiencing, so I started explaining it each time I was in the middle of something. It helped us find a cadence that slowed the pace of life. We said no to a lot of activities, events, and time with friends so we could focus on our 'new normal' and learn together as a family.

The kids learned our new routine when I arrived home from work and would grab books to sit on the couch or on the floor next to me while I took a nap. They learned to pick up on queues and recognized if I wasn't feeling well. They knew when we had to slow down, physically or when we were communicating. I wouldn't wish MS on anyone, but it helped heal our marriage and gave us tools to talk about our emotions. Now, all of us are more emotionally and physically aware of what's happening in our bodies and continue to learn how to communicate with each other.

And through all of this, life went on. Nina and I had just bought our first home, four doors down from the rental we were living in. We had moved seven times in the first six years of our marriage, so we were professionals at packing and moving with great efficiency. I knew it would take about two hours to empty the house and everyone could be back with their families by noon. We had this! However, the Tuesday before the move, I woke up with a sharp pain in my eye. It was a pain I was all too familiar with now. I had a busy day of meetings at the office, so I went to work anyway. As the meetings progressed, I noticed that I was having trouble putting sentences together. I knew what I wanted to say, but I could barely get it out. I decided to go home and call my doctor on the way. Within a few hours, a nurse was at my house to start a steroid infusion to hopefully reduce the inflammation in my body. The treatment would take five days. But we would be moving in three! Our plans had been thwarted and I needed to move quickly if the move was actually going to happen.

Group of Six

Nina, her mom, sisters, and our friends had been working on packing the house for a few weeks. It was my job to coordinate the move with the guys. Now I was beginning a treatment that would take all of my energy and strength to do anything physically.

My doctor clearly said, "No physical activity, Joe. You need to rest, literally sit on the couch and hang out with your family for the next seven to ten days."

What that meant was no carrying furniture, moving boxes, and certainly not stacking them like a life-size game of Tetris to pack as many as possible into one load. I wanted to do all those things, it was my responsibility, but I couldn't. By Wednesday, my speech was worse, my eye felt like someone had stabbed it with an ice pick, and now my left leg was starting to drag. I was a mess, both physically and emotionally. Nina and I needed to regroup.

I'm typically a good judge of when I need to ask for help. So with moving, I'd just send a text, "Hey man, can you help me move this thing?" "What's up guys, we're moving next weekend, can somebody help us? It will take a couple of hours. We'll provide breakfast and lunch." Yeah, those are pretty easy requests. But what wasn't easy was asking my friends, whom I had only known for a few months, to move my entire house without my help. That was a moment of humility for me. *Ugh, this sucks. Why won't my damn body work like it's supposed to? I don't want to have to ask these guys to move us while I sit idly by and watch.* I was embarrassed that I couldn't take care of my responsibilities and even thought about hiring a moving company so I wouldn't have to ask the guys. But we couldn't afford that. I knew I just had to bite the bullet.

I had already let the guys know that I wasn't feeling well, but they didn't quite know to what extent because I was hoping it would go away. However, on Thursday morning I knew I had to be upfront and call my friend, Aaron. "What up, man? Hey, I just wanted to give you an update on how I'm feeling." I went on to tell him what had happened over the past few days.

Then Aaron said, "Ah, Joe, I'm really sorry to hear that, man. That sucks. What do you need? How can we help?"

"Well, I need someone else to move my family. I can't do it."

"I'm on it," he said, "We'll take care of you. Oh, can we take you to dinner? One less thing to worry about." Aaron quickly set out to figure out how to get things done in two days. His wife, Becca, also brought us dinner that night and helped coordinate meals for the next few days.

When Saturday morning arrived, it was drizzling; a rarity for Phoenix. We were greeted by Aaron, Matt, and a handful of other guys with three trucks to move us. I was overwhelmed by their kindness. A group of people I barely knew gave up their Saturday morning to help my family. I had experienced this kind of kindness a few times before, but not on this scale. These men showed genuine concern for us in my most vulnerable state. I couldn't physically give anything of myself, and they didn't care. They just said, "Yes, we'll help. We'll be there. Whatever you need." That's the kind of relationship I had been longing for and wasn't sure existed. And in that moment, a group of guys, some of whom became my close friends, were living examples of the community I wanted to be a part of. They were 'my people.'

After the guys helped move my family, we were all in the Saturday night church crowd. I began to talk more with our pastor, Dave, about what was going on in our marriage. He offered a place to listen and encouraged me as I healed. As Nina and I got on better footing, I began volunteering during services and joined the leadership team with Dave, while Nina joined the worship team. We were careful not to overcommit and made our family a priority. Matt and Aaron helped support that and were the first guys I could really trust since leaving New Hope. We did small groups together, ate dinner with our families, and strengthened our roots. The next few months brought four more guys who would become part of my core group of friends that I call the Group of Six. They knew everything about the Makstons, the good, the bad, and the ugly.

A few weeks after I met Matt, he introduced me to a former college friend, Chad. He was a tall, light-skinned, lanky guy with gangly legs and arms. His wife once called him a "giraffe" on a hiking trip; it stuck with him and he embraced it. He had a signature greeting of a high five while saying, "Up Top." He made you feel like you spent your college years drinking beer and going to basketball games together. Chad and I were the leaders of our church's Saturday night service. Every week, we'd meet with Pastor Dave and the worship leader at Einstein's Bagel or Paradise Bakery to review the previous week's service. Dave would go over his message for next week, then we'd have an open discussion if anything happened with families that needed support. Chad could shoot the breeze with you and when tough decisions had to be made, he had this ability to take in all that was happening and just wait. He would show empathy and ask questions, but he'd hold his opinion until he had enough information to really process what was happening, go off and ask more questions to gain understanding, and then form his own opinion. I saw this trait when we were making decisions in leadership meetings and later in board meetings. I really appreciated that skill.

I shook hands with Parker as he walked into a Saturday night service. Parker and I quickly became friends as we started talking about work and the crazy amount of inefficiency that happens at the senior leadership level. We'd share work stories and eventually church stories about how hard it was to get things done. When I needed someone to talk to, he came second only to my dad, Joe, with whom I'd 'solve the world's problems' over a glass of cognac. Parker and I could talk strategy, tactics, and everything in between. At the end of most conversations, he'd ask, "So, what are you going to do about it?" Asking that question became Parker's signature way of helping me see what was possible. In many of our early conversations about work, Parker challenged me to consider bigger roles, to take on more responsibility, and ultimately helped me see my value to an organization. Parker would cheer me on as I talked about my successes, challenges, and frustrations. Then he'd finally ask, "So, what are you going to do about it?" Whenever he left my house – because he was always there to drink my cognac – I felt like I could do anything I set my mind to.

Parker had the opportunity to encourage me firsthand, when I started a leadership podcast. He'd say things like, "That was great...I love how you did that. You could ask deeper questions here, don't worry about throwing the person off if you ask an unscripted question. They're either going to answer it or not, it's part of the vulnerability you're trying to create." He went on to say that I have this innate ability to make the guest feel comfortable and get them to open up about their experience. This actually made me uncomfortable. So, Parker doubled down: "Most people are not willing to be that vulnerable, Joe. You are. That's what makes this conversation so great. People start to share the hard parts of themselves. So, what are you going to do about it?" He was my cheerleader, encouraging me to develop my interviewing skills and be open about my struggles as a leader, to create a space for podcast guests to do the same.

Parker and I are both dads, though I'm further along in raising mine. With him, I spoke openly about my struggle with not having a present dad growing up, how I felt so inadequate to lead my own children, and my passion for being a healthy man and a healthy dad. We found common ground in this area. Our boys had similar personalities, so I shared the good, the bad, and the ugly of my relationship with Eli when Parker would seek my advice on how to handle things with his son. I'd sit and listen as he worked through his own dad moments. We appreciated that we didn't have it all figured out, that we could be honest about it, and that we had someone to talk to without judgment. It felt good to reciprocate his encouragement as a dad and support him through the beginning of his son's teenage years.

In most areas of my life, Parker saw my potential and cheered me on. From starting a leadership podcast, to leaving a twenty-plus-year career in banking to pursue a different dream, to getting paid more, to being a dad, to learning to say no, to the healing process as I went through therapy. He was there for the big moments and told me he was proud of me. If you measure our relationship in minutes and hours, we didn't really have a lot of them together. It was mostly one-on-one, on the couch, in my living room. You could be sure there would be cognac, great stories, and the inevitable "What are you going to do about it?"

One Father's Day weekend, I was asked to give the message at church. I decided to share my story about growing up without a dad and choosing to surround myself with healthy men. When the service ended, I was at the front of the auditorium greeting people, praying with them, and listening to their 'dad' stories. I noticed a man with a buzz cut out of the corner of my eye who I was pretty sure I hadn't seen before and was clearly hanging back to talk to me.

When everyone started to clear out, he walked up and was pretty direct, "Hi, my name is Joe, too. This is my first time here. I really appreciated the message and hearing your story about not having a dad growing up." He went on to tell me about his family and how they had just moved to Phoenix after a short stint in the Peace Corps and on Capitol Hill in D.C. He had begun to see that he wanted to spend time with guys who loved Jesus and were trying to be healthy dads, and then, he asked if I'd be willing to have lunch with him. I was a little apprehensive about going to lunch with a random guy I had just met. Yet, he seemed sincere and I was curious about what he wanted. I am so glad that I said yes to that lunch.

After getting to know him better and hearing some pretty extraordinary stories about his travels, Joe paused. He said, "Hey, your story meant a lot to me. When I heard you talk about your dad and the intention you put into building relationships with men to support you, I knew you were the kind of guy I wanted to be friends with." I was honored that he heard that in my message, I just hoped my story was coherent. From that day on, Joe became a close friend. I enjoyed his stories, his passion for vulnerable people, and his humility. That, and the fact that he was a great travel buddy. He understood me, for better or worse. In fact, Joe was always a strong advocate for celebrating the fact that I was a healthy man and dad, despite my upbringing.

Each of these men encouraged me in their own way. They didn't have to be more than they already were. We loved each other well because we knew we had a choice, and we built trust and responsibility from there.

In the Makston house, it's a big deal when you turn thirteen. It consists of a trip anywhere in the continental U.S. that my kid wants to go to, a party, of course, and an evening of encouragement from our community. These evenings were a chance to celebrate who Eli and Mars are, to get advice from everyone in the room, and to give them access to trusted advisors beyond me and Nina.

After dinner, we all moved into the living room. Each person encouraged my kids, spoke to the gifts they saw in them, and then shared some advice. At the end of the evening, looking at my child with pride and many tears in my eyes, I said, "These are the people I trust. They are honest, kind, thoughtful, intelligent, and courageous people. I've learned so much from them, and I would come through for them in a heartbeat, just as they've done for me over the years. Now, they will do the same for you. If you need something that you don't feel comfortable asking or talking to me or Mom about, you can go to them. If you feel like I've gone off the rails, you can tell one of these people and they'll step in and help."

I wanted my children to know that they had a deep and wide community of men and women who cared about them. One of the reasons I valued the churches' small groups so much was to let the guys know that they didn't have to go through life alone and that there were some extraordinary people out there to do it with. You just have to put in the work to cultivate those relationships.

The Makston Code

Buying our home started to settle something in my soul. I had moved so much as a child and again in the early years of our marriage. Owning a house now anchored us to a neighborhood, a community, it gave us roots. I was so grateful for what we had that I wanted to share it with our friends and family. Our home would be a place where everyone was welcome, there would be room for you at our table, and you could serve yourself.

As the weeks turned into months, I realized something was still missing. I was still struggling with who I was as a dad and as a man. I still didn't know how to 'be good.' My insecurities would creep in as I watched the kids sleep peacefully in their beds at night. Most of the time, I realized it was the burden and honor of being a parent. Other times it was my childhood questioning who we were as Makstons. An inner voice would call out to me, *You're no better than your mom or Tom. What makes you think you're different?* I battled the voice and responded, *I am different. We're breaking the cycle of neglect, abandonment and divorce. We're Makstons.* But it made me think, *What do we stand for? How are we different?*

I remembered my friend Kent from New Hope talking about a family crest they came up with. It was part of his journey to define who his family would be as he healed from his own dad issues.

Trail running was still where I did my best thinking. I could process what was going on inside, listen to gospel music, and talk to God. During one of these runs, I had been contemplating the inner voice and Kent's crest. It got me thinking about who we were and how people would talk about the Makston name. On one of my runs one day, I asked God, "How do you want us to look? How do we want to be remembered?"

Surprisingly, He answered with extraordinary clarity. I heard, "We respect others, God's character shines in us, and we live with integrity. Respect, character and integrity."

These words ended up being our North Star, allowing us to see if we're doing well or if we needed to improve. It's also become the litmus test for how we treat others and how they treat us. We memorialized it in chalk on our dining room wall. It has started several conversations, inspired other families, and we have become known for it.

Circle the Wagons

Joe was always up for an adventure. Whether it was hiking the Grand Canyon, trying out a local dive bar, smoking clove cigarettes on a night hike, or traveling to another country to help someone build a house, he was the guy I wanted to do it with.

After I had known him for about six months, I got a text from him. "Hey, remember when you talked about going to Poland to research your family roots?"

"Yeah," I replied.

"How about building a house while you're there?" he continued.

"What? Build a house? For who?" I typed back. This was clearly a phone conversation.

Joe had been volunteering with Habitat for Humanity for the past few years. Now, he was planning to lead a trip in late 2014, and looking for people to go with him. It was a tie between Poland and Nepal. In the end, Nepal won out because of scheduling and availability.

I hadn't traveled internationally before, let alone to a third-world country. I had all these fears built up about the food, the culture, safety, and most importantly, how to pay for it. I told Joe that I'd go if I could figure out how to pay for it. He said, "All right, let's raise some money for you."

It was rare for Joe to see the downside of anything. Once he'd made the decision, he'd figured out how to do it. Raising money wasn't an obstacle for him. We planned a fundraiser, sent letters to as many friends and family as we could think of, asked our church for money, and Nina held a yard sale. By the time we were done, I had ended up raising almost twice as much money as I needed, which I used to help another person pay for some of their expenses. Joe just smiled and said, "I think we're going to Nepal."

A few months before the trip, my marriage took another hit of infidelity that I thought we were protected against. Unfortunately, Nina was still struggling with healthy boundaries with other men. We decided to separate, so she could have space to figure herself out. The kids went back and forth between my house and Nina's. It was the best we could do until we had a better understanding of what was going to happen with our marriage.

I invited the group of six to come over several times during those first few weeks. These weren't regular meetings or small group meetings. There was a weight in the air as we sat in a circle. Through tears and moments of anger, I began to unpack Nina's infidelity. In the end, I said, "I need your help." I asked the guys to walk through this with me to make sure I wasn't making rash decisions, that I was being kind to Nina and that I was making healthy choices for myself and my family. This was 'the moment' that we had all committed to many times. We had said, "If you ever need me, I'll be there. It doesn't matter what else is going on, day or night, just call."

Each of these men brought their perspective and heart for my family to the conversation. They asked hard questions. "What if Nina changes?" "Can you forgive her?" "Can you trust her?" "Do you want to divorce?" I didn't know the answer to any of these questions. They were there to probe the other parts of the story to make sure there were no unintended consequences, with as much information as possible. To slow the spinning cage of a carnival ride enough to move through the emotions. To breathe and say, "I'm okay with this decision," whatever that decision was.

Nina and I didn't make any decisions about our marriage right away. Instead, we both started therapy again, separately.

I also questioned whether I should go on the trip with Joe. I wanted to be there for my kids so they could have some stability in the home they grew up in, but I also needed a break. I was reeling from everything and didn't feel like I could make a healthy decision right now. My soul was almost dried up. If I was going to survive, time and space between what had happened could allow me to be refreshed by soaking in the care of a friend. It would strengthen my roots and fill my nostrils with the scent of creosote rain. So, Joe and I packed our bags and left for Nepal.

After arriving in Kathmandu, we made our way to the hotel for the evening. Fitted with dimly lit hallways, it had clean rooms, though sparsely decorated with only one bed. Joe and I would cozy up in bed that night, bro code in effect: "You sleep under the sheet, I'll sleep on top." It's crazy how guys are so afraid to touch each other.

The rest of the trip was full of firsts. Five of us squeezed into the back of a 1980s Nissan hatchback to eat Mexican food in another part of town. Old men tried to bike us up steep hills to visit the Monkey Temple. Then, we took a sketchy plane ride to a very small airport that would lead to our final destination. And finally, we built 65 houses with 400 international volunteers. It took five days to scrape the outer bark off enough bamboo with a dull knife to weave squares that would eventually become the base of the walls. Then, we covered them with plaster. All this work created a three-room house. Our house became a home for a family of four who no longer had to live in the slums and now had a decent place to live.

Our evenings were full of stories from the day; hearing more from the homeowners about their sweat equity, meeting local kids, letting them touch my beard because they'd never seen anything like it, and eating bananas from the fields next to the construction site. Halfway through the week, we were scheduled to eat at a restaurant in the village, where our compound was located. It was on the edge of a safari game reserve, hence, the compound part. There were elephant rides that could be taken right from the village square. As we pulled onto the main road, Joe said it would be cool to ride an elephant to dinner that night. He asked the bus driver to stop and got off. Thirty minutes later, the elephants could be heard trumpeting at the gates of the compound. Like something out of a safari movie, the guards swung the gates wide open and two elephants strolled in. Their trainers had them kneel on the grass while we climbed up their legs, grabbed their ears, and hoisted ourselves onto their backs. We rode down the middle of the road to dinner like Prince Ali from Aladdin, where the rest of the guests from our compound were waiting. We thanked the trainers, rubbed the elephants' trunks in gratitude, and went inside to eat.

Throughout the trip, I sent videos and pictures, and had quick calls with the kids to share my adventures. I missed them deeply, and Joe could tell it was wearing on me. In those moments, he just sat with me in the pain. He didn't have to say anything, just being in the room was enough. I cried about the brokenness of my family and how I had hoped the Makstons would be different from my childhood family. I had made a commitment to this amazing woman, loved the Lord and my children, and it didn't feel like it was enough. Joe reminded me of the progress I had made in so many areas of my life. I was truly a good dad and husband. I was a friend and encourager to so many men and women in our church. I had broken the cycle that had plagued my childhood family. This moment was hard, painful, and would take time to heal, but I would heal, no matter what decision Nina and I made. It didn't change the fact that I wasn't my mom or Tom. I was Joe Makston.

We soon returned to Phoenix, where Joe and the other five guys were waiting to help in any way they could.

Chad was one of the first to just show up at my house after I returned. He'd call on his way home from work to see how me and the kids were doing or would show up with ice cream and remind me what was happening sucked, but we could still enjoy this at least. Chad just listened and asked, "What do you need Joe? I'm here to help." He'd ask questions, get my opinion on things, then say it out loud to validate that's what I really meant. Ultimately, he was able to recap what had transpired, laying out the facts... and emotions. Then, he'd say, "What do you want to do about it?" It was helpful to have another person just listen, organize information, and gently ask questions to help.

As my marriage came to an end, Friday mornings with Aaron became a haven to let out the awful anger I was carrying inside that I didn't share out loud with Nina. Aaron just listened and didn't judge. He was the first person I called when I realized Nina was cheating on me.

"Hey, remember how I've continued to say something was off with me and Nina?" I spit out through tears.

"Yeah, what's up?" he replied.

"She's cheating on me with a guy from the kids' school. I'm headed home to talk with her."

He sighed, "What do you need? I'm here for you."

That moment was the culmination of years of spending time together. I knew Aaron would be there to help in any way he could. We had been through difficult things before; his youngest having heart surgery, problems at work, and friends dealing with marriage issues. This was another moment where my best friend would say, "I got you. I'm here for you. I love you" through his words and actions. Those were dark days, until they weren't. They turned into processing divorce, to healing from divorce, then to dating. Most of those conversations were on the trails of Phoenix Mountain Preserve. We celebrated in moments of joy as their peaks stretched toward the sky like waving hands. The switchbacks hugged us as we shared struggles and hopes of overcoming them. And the dirt absorbed the tears of pain, loss, and hope for something new that I couldn't quite express at the time.

I would be remiss if I didn't talk about the extraordinary wives of these men. Given the way my church community worked, the men interacted with the men and the women with the women. It wasn't strict separation, it was more of a nod to gender roles in the church and family unit. With that being said, the wives of my community were a place I felt most comfortable being myself. I'd get to know them mostly through side conversations as we stood around after church while our kids got out the last of their energy in hopes they'd fall asleep before we got home. I could compliment them on their hair, clothes, or shoes. We chatted about what they were reading or watching and how life was. They asked advice on helping dress their husbands better, gift ideas, and even said their husbands needed more time with other men. Basically, they would joke they needed a break from their man-baby. These women were an extra layer of care, love, and encouragement for me and the kids. As I went through my divorce, they'd ask about the kids and how they could support them. We were invited to dinner in the early days of our separation to alleviate the burden of doing one more thing as the kids transitioned between houses. And most of all, they looked me in the eyes and said, "You're doing a great job, Joe. Your kids will be proud of how you're handling this and leading them. This is hard."

Ashley, Joe's wife, sat next to him on their couch and cried with me as I processed therapy. She reminded me that I was God's creation and that He sees everything that is happening.

Parker's wife, Kate, sought understanding. She was a little quiet, but consistent, which I think is underrated. Whenever I'd see her, she'd ask how she could show up better for us. I'd get texts throughout the week to inquire how things went with a specific issue or how she could be praying for me. She spent extra time caring for Mars. Even though Kate didn't agree with choices Mars was making, she still wanted Mars to know they were seen and valued.

Chad's wife, Kristin, will love on you, and go to battle with you at the same time. She is fierce and will advocate for you with all her might.

Becca, Aaron's wife and Lindsay, Matt's wife, were very close to Nina before the divorce. They encouraged me through the healing process and celebrated with us in moments of joy along the way. The Makston clan spent countless meals, church services, backyard water parties, and moments of stillness in living rooms with these families. For years, I grieved not having deep connections with people that I could 'do life' with. These men and women showered refreshing drops of rain on me to strengthen my parched 'family' roots and a chance to breathe in the fragrant scent of creosote.

Final Thoughts

Nina and I were married for twelve years and it was good, until it wasn't. Between kids, church, and other friendships, our marriage stopped being the priority. Old habits turned up for Nina and unfortunately, we came to an impasse and chose to file for divorce. It took time to heal and forgive, and we made the decision early on to be strong co-parents and support the kids the best we could. Our commitment to put our children first has been the cornerstone of our lives. It was not an easy journey but we are now great friends. We celebrate and commiserate with each other, get advice, and even go on vacations together with the kids.

Growing up without a family, I often felt a profound void in my life, but the church communities I found as an adult filled those gaps with love and support. Within its embrace, I discovered a safe haven. The friends I made opened their arms and hearts, creating a warm and nurturing environment that made me feel valued and accepted. Through deep connections, they became my chosen family, sharing the vulnerable aspects of life with one another. Together, we celebrated joys and supported each other through hardships, fostering a sense of belonging that has become an integral part of my identity. Finding this, not only filled the void of a family, but it also shaped me into a person who understands the significance of community at the very core of my being.

Part Four

Finding Myself

Therapy has been a part of my life since my early twenties when I first contemplated suicide. I was in therapy through my marriage, divorce, and the next phase of my life after that. My friend Dan says, "It's okay not to be okay as long as you're doing something about it." I agree. It's okay to feel and be stuck, overwhelmed, and maybe even depressed. I've lived in all of these places at some point in my life. We don't have to live in this fake world where you pretend everything's fine while you're having a nervous breakdown inside. We all have shit and we have to work through it if we're ever going to truly be health and whole. I worked through some of my shit with my community, for other parts I leaned on my faith and conversations with pastors, but there came a time when I needed more. So I picked up my shit and sought the help of a licensed psychologist. (Ok, I'll stop saying shit now. Sorry.)

I had made appointments to meet with two different therapists and would decide which one was a good fit based on our first meetings. As I sat down in the nondescript waiting room of the first therapist one Tuesday morning, I was nervous and a little relieved that we might find out what was going on. I took the few minutes I had left to think about what I was going to say to this guy. I had been divorced for several years and had started dating again, but had recently broken up with my girlfriend. I thought I was okay with the breakup, though. Church was going well, and my friendships were healthy. However, there was still this undercurrent of anxiety. Work seemed overwhelming where I had previously excelled. I felt stuck. It had gotten to the point where I would sit and stare at my computer because I didn't know what to do. There were a lot of things I needed to do, but I couldn't get myself to physically do them. Yes, I had issues with my mom, I didn't know my dad, I was divorced, and struggled with being attracted to men. But I had already done therapy for those issues. The problems I now needed help with were all about work.

The therapist, Greg, had a beard that rivaled my own and was smartly dressed in a J Crew button-up, tan chinos, and a casual blazer. As he came up to me, he smiled and introduced himself in a soft, friendly voice. We walked back to his office and got acquainted, all part of the normal intake process. I answered the usual questions about why I was there, how he might be able to help, and what I hoped would be different when we were done. My answer was clear. Simply put, I wanted to get 'unstuck.'

Greg smiled and said, "I think I can help you with that."

As I left his office that Tuesday afternoon, I knew I didn't need to see the other therapist, Greg was my guy. I felt comfortable with him, I felt better just by being in the room with him.

Greg and I spent weeks building a trusting relationship. He'd ask how the work was going, and when we got to an overwhelming part of it, he'd stop me and ask where I felt it in my body. Then we would take time to just sit in that moment. This was extremely uncomfortable, it made me feel like my body was vibrating inside. But Greg explained that this discomfort was just my brain trying to settle. After hearing my origin story, Greg concluded that I was in a constant state of survival and didn't know how to let the emotion resolve. He then explained the brain science at work in each of my childhood stories.

I had been doing research on brain science for a program at work myself. This created a moment of kinship between us and we geeked out for a few minutes. Then, we went through some exercises that I could use during the week when I felt overwhelmed again and wrapped up for the day. Those exercises, plus the understanding of what was going on inside, helped me understand what my body was doing because of my trauma. It made me feel better to know that I wasn't broken, that I just needed to build coping skills to deal with my trauma. It wasn't about work, which was the path of least resistance for the emotions to come out. Yes, I needed to find balance to get 'unstuck,' but this was core healing that needed to happen.

One modality Greg used is Internal Family Systems (IFS). This is a fascinating stuff, and I encourage everyone to read more about it. Simply put, IFS focuses on the different parts of ourselves that have helped us function in (early) life.

One of these parts may have been established during a traumatic event and continues to function at the development level you were at when it happened, even as your physical body continues to grow. To give myself space to interact with these parts, we used visual imagery, a kind of inner world. Most of this world was filled with lush fields of grass, a forest with rivers, a lake, and mountains. By using this imagery, I could talk to the different parts (ages) of myself and acknowledge how they had kept us safe. I could also celebrate what a great job they had done. These exercises helped me understand those times when I had been scared, stressed, feeling shame, pride, or really any other emotion and to get to know the inner children at different ages who were trying to manage those emotions.

Think about a six-year-old who is trying to manage their emotions when somebody is yelling at them. That's how I felt inside, because the part of me that came up to protect me when someone was yelling had never developed beyond that age. I hadn't healed from the trauma of my mom constantly yelling at me whenever I didn't do something exactly the way she wanted me to. That is why even now when someone yells at me, I become a six-year-old in a forty-year-old body. This understanding allowed me to separate my trauma from who I was as a person.

For most of my life, I thought there was something inherently wrong about me, that I had "be good," and that I must have done something wrong for people to keep walking away.

Greg would ask me where in my body I felt this. He'd say, "Let's just acknowledge it. We don't have to do anything with it. Just be aware of it."

We'd sit for a few minutes. Then he'd check in on me, asking if it was worse, the same, or better. Depending on the day, it could be any of those things. Whenever he asked me how I felt, I described it as being in a dark, foggy room. It felt like we were revisiting that room over and over again.

During the week, I would spend time repeating the words Greg had said, "Just acknowledge it. We don't have to do anything." Then the feeling would slowly start to pass.

When another visit with Greg began, I was in the fog again. But this time, as we sat in the emotion of it, the fog began to gather in one place, giving way to the rest of the room. I could hold it in my hand, like a black ball. The fog represented my experiences of neglect, abandonment, abuse, not feeling wanted, loss of hope, and shame. Now I could see that these were things that had happened to me, but they didn't define who I was. I had been neglected and abandoned by my mom, yes. I had been physically, sexually and emotionally abused, yes. The challenges was mine, but it was not me; they don't define who I am. I am a loving dad, a good friend, a strong leader, an encourager, compassionate, and brave. The image of holding the black ball of all that trauma allowed me to distance myself so that I could actually see it from the outside instead of being in it. That's when we started using the language of "It's mine, but it's not me." I could finally see that part of myself and not be overwhelmed by the fog of my childhood.

Over the next year or so, we resolved the work issue, then moved through the issues with Mom, Tom, and even the remnants of my divorce. We gave these different 'parts' of my inner child space to express themselves, to grieve, to celebrate their work, and to begin to heal. By understanding why they existed and how to release them from managing parts of my life, I, the whole Joe, was able to reassure the younger parts that we were going to be okay. I used the exercises Greg taught me to learn how to release emotions.

My mind felt freer, clearer, and I began to take care of the 'parts' that needed reassurance that we weren't going to be in the places that traumatized them so long ago. These younger parts still occasionally step in when I realize that I, the whole Joe, am not fully present or I'm triggered, and they try to take over. However, I'm more aware of when this happens and to take more time to sit with what's going on, asking myself and the 'part' questions to allow it to process. The result is that I feel the heart of the matter, there's shame, fear, anger, and loneliness.

I had to learn to give myself enough grace to acknowledge that these emotions were okay to sit with. I had spent so much time trying to 'be good' and follow the rules that I couldn't show myself love when a part of me was struggling. The time with Greg helped me to see how I needed to show myself grace, love, and self-care. I didn't have to explain it or get permission from anyone else. It was about taking care of these little children that were living in my inner world.

Desolate Place

Most of the landscape in my inner world looked like northwest Washington: red cedar and fir trees reaching to the clouds, the soil full of organisms and decaying leaves and pine needles – rich and earthy and refreshing. You can move about freely, the air feels crisp, and there is a cleansing mist from The Sound. The canopy arches over you, filtering the sun to give way to shards of light glimmering through the branches. It's safe, comforting, and inviting.

In-between sessions with Greg, I spent time in these landscapes, talking to the different parts of myself that we had just met or were struggling with. One of the skills Greg had taught me was to pause, visualize the collective group of children in my mind, and ask , "Does anyone have anything they want to talk about?" I'd give that part of me space to share, and I'd process it as whole-self Joe or with Greg the next time we were together. But there was still a voice calling out, one that wasn't with the others. I was afraid of it, I had pushed it to the back of my mind so I wouldn't have to face it.

There was another part of my inner world that I never went to, I tried to actually forget about it. It looks a bit like a stretch of desert between Phoenix and Tucson. In late July, when it hasn't rained in months, the ground is cracked, sunk in, longing for a drop of rain to relieve the relentless beating of the sun. There is hardly any shade and dust devils suck up dirt across the flat land. Even a moment in the shade of an occasional rock formation offers little protection from the heat or the sun.

There were the things I was ashamed of, and insecure about. God and the Holy Spirit had access to every other part of my life, but I couldn't bear opening that door. I had spent a lifetime separating these parts of my life from everything else in order to prove that I was good, that I followed the rules, and that I was a confident, Christian man. These were the parts of me that I had pushed out into the Tucson desert of my childhood, hoping they would die.

But as I came to terms with the children in the lush green forests, Greg and I decided that we needed to start exploring the desert as well.

In the distance, a rock formation appears through the radiant heat waves vibrating from the ground. Hoping to catch a moment of respite, I move toward it. The formation rises out of the parched land, giving way to the entrance of a cave. This place feels familiar, and the pit in my stomach bubbles up to my chest as my heartbeat increases. I know this place. Wait, there is something in there. I hear its groans, its heavy breathing as it begins to stir, knowing that I am just outside. My feet will not take me further than the entrance. I can feel the heat coming from inside the cave, and my hope of resting in its coolness shrivels like thirsty desert plants. Fear and curiosity tug at my mind and I start moving again. The familiarity of what is in there draws me in, despite the fear of what is about to confront me. Just around the first corner of the cave, all light from outside is cut off, and I stand in total darkness. I remember that I have a flashlight on a keychain in my pocket. I pull it out to find my way deeper into the darkness. The sliver of light that protrudes barely allows me to see the next step in front of me.

Greg and I spent a few weeks traveling to The Desolate Place and entering the cave to try to make our way further inside. The tiny light I was using made it difficult, though. By the third week I was frustrated; why was it taking so long? I had started healing in so many places, but this place scared me.

One day, Greg decided to take me back to an earlier exercise of just sitting in the emotion of what I was feeling, allowing the fear to rise and fall in the moment. I asked myself questions about why I couldn't go further into the cave and what was in there that I didn't want to see. Often, I would ask the Holy Spirit to come and be with me. But whatever was inside, didn't want the Holy Spirit there. By the time I realized this, I had reached the end of our appointment, so the 'why' would have to wait.

For the next few days, I couldn't get it out of my mind. Being a Christian and understanding who the Holy Spirit is, I should be totally okay with this. But it was a hard "stop, do not pass go, do not collect two hundred dollars." As I spent more time thinking about my fears, the heat I had felt from inside the cave gave way to beasts that lurked in the corners and began to take shape. Out of fear, I had banished parts of myself to the lethal desert.

Until I reached my forties, I had a skewed perspective of who God was. I had always viewed Him like the Statue of Abraham Lincoln in the Lincoln Memorial in Washington DC. This towering figure was observing from a distance, overseeing all that was happening, and too large to connect with. He was up there somewhere. He knew about me, but didn't really want to interact. Even after the experience in my twenties when I was looking for my dad, I was still kind of scared of Him. I had made God bigger than He really was.

At church that weekend, we were in the middle of singing and I was still distracted. How could I face the beasts waiting for me in the cave? I had forced them there, and now they had spent my lifetime trying to survive in terrible circumstances. My focus flowed between singing songs and back to the beasts. Then suddenly, with a moment of clarity, it was as if the largest beast, called out from a distant, desolate place.

"Talk about me," it whispered, "what does God think of me?"

I knew that voice, it was the one I had been pushing away since I was a kid. Why was it speaking now, in church? It knew there was no place for it here. I tried to ignore the voice, but it kept pushing.

In a crowded room, with hundreds of people singing to the Lord, I took a breath and finally found the confidence to ask God, "Can we talk about being gay?"

In the same soft, comforting voice I heard so many years ago as I pulled a Bible verse card off my windshield, God spoke. As if He were standing next to me, He said, "Yes. I've been waiting for you to ask."

The room went silent and drops of rain began to penetrate the dry, dusty ground of my heart, showering it with hope. The guarded half-breath that held the courage to ask God *that* question was now a full, deep sigh of relief. I had lived with the belief that there was a special place in hell for those who were gay, and you couldn't be that and be a Christian. In reality, God was saying, "I love you. You are important. There's nothing wrong with you." *What the hell... how was that true? Were there other parts of me that God loved that I didn't? I wasn't the horrible beast I had built myself up to be?* When I let go of how I thought He would judge me and stopped believing the lie that I would never be good enough, He instantly transformed into someone *beside* me. He wanted to be in every part of my life and it was ok if it was messy. God became someone I could walk with, talk to and trust with the deepest parts of myself. I couldn't wait to go to therapy with Greg on Tuesday. I even texted him on Monday to share what I was realizing.

When I arrived at Greg's office on Tuesday, I was anxious to get started. I had been waiting to process what had happened over the weekend. I shared the highlights of what I was realizing and Greg suggested that we approach The Desolate Place to see what happened.

The weekend experience had helped me understand that the Holy Spirit needed permission to go into the cave with me. I had spent decades pushing these parts into the desert, now it was time to face the beast, along with the Holy Spirit. Although I was a little afraid of what would come next, the beasts hiding in the cave were willing to let the Holy Spirit come in. My penlight turned into a flashlight beam, revealing a guy resembling a misfit toy from Toy Story and a scaly beast guarding access to the rest of the trapped outcasts. As the light in the cave grew brighter, I saw that the beasts I'd assumed were there to harm me were only children, like the Lost Boys of Neverland. In order to survive and give up their childhood, they had created larger-than-life characters to be brave and protect themselves. These characters established their own set of rules, practices, and attitudes, only to bring harsh judgments and consequences upon each other. Each time I visited the Desolate Place, it was a chance to talk to those parts of myself and understand what they had experienced. It was as if they were frozen in time, functioning at the age they were when they had experienced the trauma.

The Desolate Place is a reminder of the things I couldn't love about myself: my abandonment issues, not feel I belonged, body dysmorphia, and being gay. These parts of me believed that they couldn't be loved and that they were probably why people kept leaving. But that wasn't true! It took months of visiting this place and processing the pain of my childhood to free myself from the harsh judgments and lies they believed. Part of the therapy was figuring out how to integrate these pieces and learn not to emotionally function as a child. IFS equipped me with the skills I needed to heal, cope, and recognize when a part of me needs something or understand why I might feel a certain way.

These are truly only children fighting the battles of my childhood and they were waiting to be told how proud I was of the work they've been doing to keep us alive. I told them the story of where we are today. They were freed from carrying the torch as I moved towards becoming my whole self. None of the younger parts of me live in The Desolate Place anymore. They are part of who I am, have begun to heal, and reside in the lush landscape of my inner world. They are sometimes complicated, but shown immense grace, and love. As I began to do this consistently, I was brave enough to look Greg in the eyes, through a Zoom call, and say, "I'm gay." He sat with me in silence while tears streamed down my face. It was like I could truly breathe for the first time.

Rocky Road

I have one last story to tell you about how this newfound wisdom manifested in my life. This story is about Justin, the last of the group of six. During this phase of my life, I was mostly in church and I met most of my friends there. Justin could shoot the breeze with me, then jump into the deep end with a level of honesty that I didn't experience very often. We went through a few years where we didn't see much of each other, as he was finishing his nursing practitioner program, had little kids at home, and was part of a different church. When I started therapy, I decided to take a break from leading everything at church. I didn't have the energy to manage myself and support other men. When I took a break, Justin and I decided we still wanted to spend time together so we talked about what seemed reasonable given everything he had going on.

"Hey bud, I know I'm really busy and I'd love to have regular time with you," he shared.

"Yeah, I'd totally be down with that J." I said in agreement.

I already had a hiking buddy in Aaron, went on adventures with Joe, and 'solved the world's problems' with Parker, so Justin and I needed to find our thing.

Justin had an idea of what he was looking for, "With how crazy my job is, I just needed to decompress and veg out. Like watching a 'man show' on Netflix. Something totally mindless, so we can talk and not really worry about being invested in what's actually happening. Oh, and we should eat ice cream."

I was in immediately.

The next week, at 7:45PM, I got a text from Justin, "Kids down, on my way buddy. Do you have ice cream?"

When he got to my place, we scooped out copious amounts of rocky road and mint chocolate chip ice cream, sat on the couch and talked about life. After about thirty minutes, we turned on a show and just chilled. We didn't need to talk, just to be in the same room together. We knew we cared deeply and chose to love and trust one another. No judgment, just love and support.

Several years before, I had told Justin that I struggled with same-sex attraction when I was younger so he already knew part of my story. But as I got into the deep end of therapy, I needed space to share some of the emotions I was feeling. What's more, I needed to test out everything going on in my brain. The time Justin and I had been spending together was the safe space I needed. We already spent time catching up and spoke about some pretty tough stuff between the ice cream and the 'man show'. It took a long time to get up the nerve, though.

Sitting on my couch while catching up on the past week, with ice cream in hand, I mustered the nerve to say, "There are some things I think I'm starting to figure out with my therapist that I wanted to tell you."

"Sure man, what is it?" he said.

I paused, considering the risk that saying this out loud could change our friendship forever.

Noticing my apprehension Justin said, "Dude, I've seen some crazy ass shit in my work. Whatever you have to say, there's no way I'm going to be freaked out by it. It's alright man. Lay it on me."

I dove head-first into it: "I'm pretty sure I'm gay."

He asked me a few questions which I answered as best as I could. Then, he looked at me and said, "It doesn't change how I feel about you. I love you and you're my friend."

We ate some more ice cream and watched another episode of 'Shooter' on Netflix.

That night was transformational in my relationship with Justin and set the groundwork for how I hoped the other guys would respond. I could freely share the pain I was healing from, deconstruct life and the expectations I had created for myself, and explore the fears about what people may think if I actually was gay. He reassured me he wasn't going anywhere and would love me for who I was as a person, not who I chose to be with.

As I said goodbye to Justin that evening, he gave me a tight hug and reaffirmed his love for me. I told him it was ok to tell his wife Roseann, I was going to need all the support I could get over the next several months. Roseann basically became a little sister to me, including all the joking, annoyance, competitiveness, and care a little sister brings to the relationship. She liked to get to the real issue and wasn't afraid to ask questions. She had deep empathy for me and what this meant for my relationships at church. Just like Ashley, Joe's wife, she sat with me and Justin as I unpacked my story through tears. Their unwavering presence by my side provided a comforting assurance that I was not alone. They approached the situation with genuine care and affection, treating me like family. Their continuous reminders of love helped me find strength and acceptance in my own identity.

Final Thoughts

I attribute the man I am today to Greg's skill as a clinician and my willingness to do the work and the foundation we laid during the four years we were together. I stand as a testament to the transformative power of healing. The journey was arduous, but it allowed me to confront the deep-rooted pain and wounds that had haunted me for so long. Through this process, I experienced tremendous growth and began to accept the 'parts' I didn't think were worthy of love. I learned to love myself unconditionally, embracing both the light and dark within me. When I got out of my own head and shared what was really going on, I set myself up to be a healthy man and dad. Many tears were shed and my children had seen me both at the bottom of a deep depression and also witnessed the work of healing. That doesn't mean I don't have bad days. Four decades of habits and trauma cannot be healed in four days, months, or even years. I'm okay with the slow process.

Gratitude fills my heart as I reflect on the friends who stood by me throughout this healing journey. They offered their unwavering presence, empathy, and understanding during my darkest moments. With their support, I felt safe to confront my past traumas and explore the depths of my emotions. Their love and encouragement reminded me that I was worthy of healing and happiness. Their belief in me and their willingness to hold space for my pain created a nurturing environment for me to grow and thrive. I am forever grateful for their support and will cherish their friendship as a precious gift.

Closing

I'm proud of who I am today. I am a dad, friend, brother, son, leader, good listener, a bit of a smartass, Christian, and gay. This is just the beginning of who I am. I am convinced that to be a healthy, loving, others-focused human, I needed a combination of community, therapy, and faith. If one component was missing, it was easy for things to go sideways. When I solely used faith, but no therapy, I didn't clearly understand why I was struggling and was not equipped to be whole. Without faith, I would miss the knowledge that I was here to do something greater than myself and wouldn't have had the strength to carry on. Lastly, without community, it's a lonely life. I would have missed out on the opportunity to share my life with others and to learn from theirs. I am still a work in progress and so are these three areas of my life. I now know I need to be gracious with myself and thoughtful in how I approach each one.

In my quest for home, family, and belonging, I needed to heal and accept who I was before I could really understand the community I wanted to be part of. The Makstons, Bartos, and Hamacks will always be part of my given family. I get to decide who my chosen family is. The goal is to build a healthy community that is best for me and my family. I'm still discovering both who I am and who I'm not, and learning what and who I stand for. We are still bound together by the Makston Code: respect, character, and integrity. This is who we continue to be as a family, although we look very different than we did in the early years. We are better for it. We have learned to love in the hard places, to laugh out loud, to praise each other, and to suffer in pain together.

Authenticity and vulnerability were two of the greatest gifts I received from my friend, Pastor Dan. It's hard to tell parts of my story. I may share the pain of loss, the shame of not loving myself, and the embarrassment of being judged. But when I've had the opportunity to share who I was and who I'm becoming, more people thank me than judge me. I think God wants people to know that they're not alone, that there's someone they can relate to and live with and be whole with.

Now, when I visit Tucson, surrounded by its rich desert landscape, I can't help but stop and look at the scenery. Whether it's summer or spring (because, come on, we don't have the other two seasons), there is beauty in the desert brush, the cacti, and Mt. Lemmon reaching for the sky. As monsoon clouds roll over the mountains and thunder crackles in the distance, I close my eyes to take in the smell of creosote. The rain is coming. Droplets of life will soon wash away weeks of dust blown back and forth, collect on tiny leaves, soak into the parched ground, and make their way to the roots to replenish a parched soul.

As the thunder comes closer, I feel the first drops brush my face as they make their way to the ground. The wind begins to pick up, first warm and stale, then cooling and carrying a hint of creosote. Tiny drops turn into larger ones, which now begin to cover me and the dry earth beneath my feet. I stretch our my arms, tilt my head to the sky and let the rain penetrate the rest of my face, tapping against my skin. I feel the nourishment of a life that once withered in silence. The rain strengthens my soul, bringing to life the true Joe who has been hiding for too long. The desert, which spends most of its life in a quiet, reserved, survival mode, is now bursting with life.

That was the picture of my life: knowing only how to sustain myself long enough until the next rain came. The people who encouraged, supported and loved me were my saving grace. My community gave me hope that I could be accepted; my faith showed me that there had to be more to this life and that I should share my story; and therapy strengthened my roots to know that I mattered and belonged. I now feel whole and lovable. I am no longer this abandoned and abused child forced to hide in a desolate place. I am Joe Makston – whole, loved, and accepted.

Epilogue

Well, that was quite an adventure. Please allow the car to come to a complete stop before exiting the ride. Thanks for coming along with me. There are a few loose ends I wanted to tie up here.

Kathy – Mom – still lives in Tucson, in a 55+ mobile home park. She has a few friends who regularly meet at the clubhouse to eat together and talk about their week. Over the past few years, I have been able to have meaningful conversations with my mom. With the complexity of mental health issues and her personality, it can sometimes be difficult to communicate with her. We can talk about how she's doing, and I share parts of my life with her because she's been able to show up differently. Once I was able to recognize how she communicates and how she shows love, even when she is stressed, it was easier to reset my expectations. We're still figuring out how to love and encourage the people we are. My relationship with her remains the same: it has solid boundaries with enough room to check in on each other for her to catch up on what's going on with my siblings, and for me to talk about the kids and work. Sis moved into the same trailer park to make sure Mom had the support she needed as she continued to age.

Tom – When I was in my thirties, Tom had a stroke that eventually led him to move to Dallas where my brother Pat lived. So I would see him when I went to visit Pat and his family. Tom was kind and genuinely interested in my life. I knew he was trying to connect with me, but too much of life had passed and the wounds were too deep. I chose to be polite and show kindness in return, but he remained a stranger to me. Tom passed away in 2017 after complications from several medical conditions.

The Sibs – I'm still very close to Pat, Pennie and Sis. We have a shared experience with Mom at the center. Each of us have gone through years of therapy to heal and be better. When we're all in the same place, which is rare, the room is filled with joy, laughter, cursing, smoked meat from Pat, and enough love for each other to know we're going to be okay. We still follow the Carnie Code and will show up for each other at a moment's notice, and we know how to get rid of the bodies. We talk to each other every month and a half or so. If something happens that we all need to know about, we use a text thread called 'The Sibs'. It can be anything from pictures of the family, important issues that have come up that we honestly don't want to have to call everyone separately, or an update on Mom so we can all be in agreement or help Sis, since she's at ground zero with her.

After Pennie moved to Minnesota in 2005, she came out as a lesbian. She still lives in Minnesota with her partner. Her kids are scattered across three different states. Sis currently lives in Arizona, but spent most of her adult life outside of Dallas, close to my brother, Pat. Pat lives outside of Dallas with his family, his wife, Heather, and three boys.

Aunt Darlene – We don't see each other much these days. She did the heavy lifting when I was in high school and college. When I got married, she knew I had a good foundation. She loved her own adventures and looked forward to functioning independently. We still care for each other and reminisce about old times when we're together. When my brother is in town, he usually gets us all together. Aunt Darlene still lives in Glendale, AZ.

Nina – We live three blocks away from each other and talk almost every day. We have had to work through some painful crap to get to where we are today. Nina is one of my closest friends and a fierce ally. She's still doing hard shit as a certified mountain rescue volunteer, hiker, and runner. We enjoy doing things together as a family, whether it's family game nights, dinners, holidays, or just the two of us eating together. It scares the kids a little bit, which makes the friendship even better. I have deep respect for Nina, her story, and how she came out the other side a better person.

Eli & Mars – I have the honor of being the dad of these two. They make it easy to choose time with them over working sixty hours a week. Eli is a brilliant tech kid, vocally gifted and perpetually curious, with a compassionate heart for the people around him. Mars has an innate ability to see underrepresented communities and strives to give them a voice. Mars is also gifted in the arts, including painting, drawing, pottery, acting, and she prefers classical over contemporary singing. Eli and Mars continue to approach life with humility in order to serve others. Whether it's a zip-lock bag of necessities for the homeless, hanging out with kids, or going to Mexico to show love to people. Both have a heart to help people feel part of a community.

Cookies are our love language; we spent the first year of the pandemic perfecting the Makston chocolate chip cookie. One of our favorite pastimes is singing in the car. Even when there is conflict and the kids are 'being kids,' there is something about music that connects us. It is usually Broadway show tunes. We can belt out songs from Hamilton, Beetlejuice, Dear Evan Hanson, Wicked, or Waitress. We still love to see houses decorated with Christmas lights and yell: "MERRY CHRISTMAS" as we drive by.

When the kids were little, I chose to be a healthy man and dad so they could have a different story than I had. I want to be fully present for them, to be an advocate, to help them cultivate their voices. There are days when I fail, and they are quick to forgive me and move on. We try to find common ground and choose to ask questions to understand each other instead of being judgmental. They are constantly teaching me about life and their culture. As parents, our goal was to raise humble, decent people, and I think we've done a good job so far. It's truly one of my greatest joys to be their dad.

The Bartos – I still see Mom and Dad regularly, but not as much as I would like. When we went to church together, it was easy to grab lunch afterwards to catch up. Now, we have to be very intentional. Even though they don't agree with me being gay, they continue to be respectful and loving, and occasionally Dad would ask how my partner is doing. That's all I can ask of them. We all have boundaries and values that align or create separation. It's the way we approach it all with curiosity, grace, and trust that makes the difference. I really enjoy getting together with Dad to 'solve the world's problems.' When too much time has passed, I missed his encouraging words, his laughter, his curiosity, his wisdom, and his pure love for me. We are quick to text to say hi and try to get together over our favorite pastime, food. Even when the conversations were difficult and I finally came out to him, he was true to his word when he said, "I love you. I'm not going anywhere. You're my son."

Community – Well, this looks very different now than it did for most of my life. Before therapy, the only friends I had were from church. After I gained the confidence to be my whole self and come out, my church asked me to leave because I was no longer in line with their beliefs. Although this was heartbreaking, I was strong enough to separate my identity as a healthy gay man from the shame that had been placed on me. The 'Group of Six' guys reacted in different ways. Two drew a hard line in the sand and told me we couldn't be friends anymore. Since we all went to church together, I rarely see the ones who wanted to stay because there isn't this natural cadence built in. I've learned to hold relationships loosely because they may only be there for a season. I think community is an organism and should evolve. It shouldn't look the same as it did last year, though it's a lot easier to write about this than to live it. As I've begun to rebuild my community, I've chosen to be friends with people who expose and challenge me to new ideas, beliefs, cultures, and political views. We don't always agree, but we respect and care for each other.

Faith – I had a bit of a faith crisis while writing this book. My views on organized religion are very different now. But this hasn't stopped me from connecting with God. I still have a need to feel accepted by others and really want to write a long statement to validate my relationship with Him. But I'm not going to do that. I have a deep love for the God of the universe. My relationship with Him is personal, purposeful, and real. I live with the conviction that it's essential to love God and others. I now have the freedom to love someone with their differences, whatever they may be. I couldn't say that a few years ago, and I'm still learning. I think that's the point, we shouldn't have it all figured out. God wants me to keep growing and I'm going to keep asking Him, "Help me understand how to love and see this person the way you do." That's good enough for me and I think it's good enough for Him, too.

About the Author

Joe Makston is a seasoned professional with over twenty years of experience in the banking industry. He then entered the technology space to lead learning & development and employee experience centers of excellence. However, it is his passion for leadership development that truly sets him apart. Joe has dedicated himself to nurturing and empowering individuals to reach their full potential, believing in the transformative power of leading self, leading others and leading together.

In addition to his career, Joe has been a podcaster, TEDx speaker, and is an accomplished author. He co-wrote a book titled "Tummy Tales: Questions with My Dad" alongside Mars, capturing the heartwarming bond between a father and child. Joe continues to share his own personal story and encourages others to share theirs, recognizing the power of vulnerability and the building of genuine connections. His passion for storytelling serves as a catalyst for authentic communities where individuals feel seen, heard, and supported.

Joe resides in North Central Phoenix, with his kids and two dogs, Olive and Scout. He enjoyed running and mountain biking on the vast mountain trails in the Phoenix area.

Instagram: @jmakston
Facebook: Joe Makston
LinkedIn: joe makston